Teachers' T of the Trade

Everything you ever wanted to know about teaching but were afraid to ask

Elizabeth Gwilliams

Please note that throughout this book we have referred to the child as 'he'; the class teacher as 'she' and the Headteacher as 'he' **merely for convenience**. In no way do we mean to imply that this is the norm.

Author: Elizabeth Gwilliams,
         Deputy Head of White Notley C.E. Primary School, Essex.

Illustrator: Maggie Ling

Longman Group UK Limited,
Longman House,
Burnt Mill, Harlow,
Essex, CM20 2JE, England
and Associated Companies throughout the world.

First published 1991
Fourth impression 1994

Set in 10/12 pt Optima

Produced by Longman Singapore Publishers Pte Ltd
Printed in Singapore

The publisher's policy is to use paper manufactured from sustainable forests.

Contents

Preface

I know introductions are boring so I shall be as brief as possible but there are some things I felt I ought to mention before you read this book.

This book is not meant to be read from cover to cover like a novel. Most teachers haven't time for that luxury and when they do they don't want to read a book about teaching! This book is meant to be used as a resource. Use the bits you like and leave those that don't appeal to you. This is not a how-to-do-it book but a this-worked-for-me-so-why-don't-you-try-it-too? book.

A teacher's job changes from day to day, from class to class and from child to child. This is part of the challenge of the profession. There is no definitive way to teach and this book would not set itself up as such. But teaching is often an isolated task and we are left to fall back onto our own resources. Over the years we begin to know what will work and what won't. This experience is of great value to the individual teacher. Nothing can really replace the knowledge gained by years at the 'chalkface' but I hope that this book will pass on some of the ideas and tradecraft that I have learnt in my years of teaching or were handed down to me by older and wiser colleagues.

Talking of older and wiser colleagues, I must express my thanks to the staff of White Notley Primary School for their help and support while I researched this book and to the children on whom I try to practise what I preach.

Elizabeth Gwilliams

Applying for a Teaching Post

There are basically three ways of finding a teaching post.

1 Newspaper advertisements

The newspapers which carry most of the job vacancies nationally are the *Times Educational Supplement* (affectionately known as the 'TES') and *The Teacher*. The local newspaper for your area will carry advertisements for local teaching vacancies.

2 Local Authority Circulars

Most local authorities advertise vacancies on a circular which is distributed regularly to schools and other educational establishments. Sometimes posts will be only advertised this way and not in the national press. If you are looking for a post in a new area it can sometimes be worthwhile writing to the County Hall of the area in which you wish to teach and asking them to post you a copy of the county circulars as they are published. You will need to enclose enough stamped addressed envelopes for the period of time you are job hunting. Some counties will not do this and you will need to find someone who can copy the circular for you, either from a school or from the copy available for general perusal at County Hall.

3 The Grapevine

It is a well-known phenomenon that Headteachers would rather employ someone they know or that someone they know knows, than advertise for a complete stranger. Often posts are advertised by word of mouth 'Do you know anyone who would like a term's contract?' before the official advertisement is placed. Therefore it is a wise move when job hunting to go on the supply list or to volunteer to help out at a local school.

Advertisements vary tremendously and, like estate agency details, you need to be able to read between the lines. Often Headteachers will list the ideal qualities they would like in their new teacher. Many of these qualities are not absolutely necessary and basically they are looking for a competent classroom teacher. Phrases to look out for are:
  ▷ ability to teach music preferred

▷ ability to teach throughout the age-range preferred

▷ science or PE would be an advantage

If you are in any doubt, telephone the Headteacher to find out how serious is his need for a musician/science teacher etc. Most Headteachers are happy to talk to candidates this way and you could save yourself from a lot of time and heartache, applying for a post for which you were not suitable.

In some advertisements the Headteacher is looking for a teacher with specific skills. In this case the wording will be more definite:

▷ must have sympathy with child-centred education

▷ will be expected to teach music throughout the school and must be a competent pianist

▷ should have a strong commitment to games and be willing to organise teams

One last word of warning; if an advertisement states that the candidate should be able to take boys' games this may imply that the school would prefer to employ a male teacher.

Your next step is to send off for an application form and to prepare your letter of application. It is also wise to look around the school at this stage. You may find that having looked around the school you do not wish to apply for the post. If you look around the school and then apply, the Headteacher then knows that you really wish to work in his school and not just any school in the area.

It is preferable to fill in the application form in black ink using block capitals. This makes the form look neater and easier to read. Black also photocopies well. If possible your letter of application should be typed. It is neater and means you can write more in a limited space. Try to adapt your letter of application so that it meets the needs of the school.

Often application forms may not include other details you may wish the Headteacher to know. It can do no harm if you include your curriculum vitae with your application form. You can cover yourself by including a sentence in your letter of application such as:

'I enclose my curriculum vitae for your further interest.'

Your curriculum vitae should be typed and it is easier if details which will have to be updated are on a separate sheet. An example curriculum vitae is included in the *Appendices* on p142.

Interviews

It is important to remember that interviews are a two-way affair. You are appraising the school as a place of work as much as the headteacher/governors are appraising you as a candidate for their teaching vacancy.

Interviews are an opportunity for the Headteacher and governors to meet you as a person. On paper you must be suitable for the post because you have received the offer of an interview. Viewed in this light if you are not offered the post you should not view yourself as a failure. You may have a lot to offer a school but your particular character strengths are not perhaps what this school was looking for. The candidates who are not offered the post often consider themselves inferior to the candidate who is offered the post. This is usually untrue. Everyone is different and the Headteacher chooses someone with qualities which he feels are best suited for that vacancy and school. Another Headteacher may have different priorities.

The best time to assess the school as a suitable place for you to work is when you are being shown round. Obviously you will have made sure that you are able to fit in with the teaching style of the school but here are some other areas for consideration as to whether the school might be best avoided.

1 Why did the last holder of the post leave?

2 What is the turnover of staff? Happy staff tend to stay put. However there may be a very genuine reason why there are suddenly six vacancies at one school.

3 Is the Headteacher welcoming? friendly? stern? absent-minded? A school tends to reflect the character of its Headteacher.

4 Is the Headteacher enthusiastic about the school and its children? What is the Headteacher's relationship with his staff and children?

5 What is the physical appearance of the school? Although it may not be well-maintained because of the financial problems of the LEA has there been some effort made to make best use of the buildings? Is there any graffiti? Is it clean and tidy?

6 What are the school resources like? Are they well cared for even if limited? Has the school the same priorities as yourself or are they spending half of their capitation on PE equipment?

7 Look at the work on the walls. Is it of a reasonable standard? How long has it been there?

8 What is the stock situation? How is it allocated?

9 How friendly are the staff? What do they say about the school? Are they positive about the school or full of shaded warnings?

10 What are the school dinners like?

An interview is a very stressful situation and you obviously want to show yourself in a good light. Here are some ideas which may help.

1 Wear something smart, but comfortable. Men will need to wear a suit. Try to wear natural fibres in case you perspire when you become nervous.

2 When you are shown around the school aim to make only one intelligent comment. Don't prattle on about how you agree with everything you see including their choice of Maths/Language/Science scheme. The Headteacher may be new and has inherited a scheme he hates. Use the time to listen to what your guide is telling you about the school. You may pick up some interesting information you can use to your advantage in your interview.

3 Take a book to read or something to do in case there are six other candidates and your name begins with a Z.

4 When people come out of a stressful situation they like to talk. Listen carefully to what the other candidates say about their interview and mentally prepare dynamic answers to questions which obviously floored them.

5 Be yourself in the interview. Don't be too poker faced. Smile occasionally! If you can, lighten your answers without being flippant.

6 Don't sit too rigidly. Keep hands still and men try not to sit in the position with your foot resting on your thigh/knee.

7 Give all questions equal attention — even obviously daft questions from inexperienced governors.

8 Give yourself a few moments to think before you answer any question. What may seem like a harrowing silence to you is probably only a few seconds and a well-thought out answer is better than an immediate ramble.

9 When answering a question try to show that you know the general theory and then give specific (preferably practical) examples.

10 Don't have prepared set answers — it always shows.

11 Don't give the answer you think that they want to hear.

12 Don't ask a question at the end of the interview unless your acceptance of the post depends upon the answer.

Starting a new job

After your interview may be the only time you have to discuss your new post before the beginning of the new school year. If this is so then you will be introduced to the person who is leaving and you will need to get all the relevant information you can from them before you leave. However after the stress of the interview it is very easy to overlook something important.

You will have many questions about the school and its routine which should be answered by the school's Staff Handbook — ask for a copy if you are not given one. Other things you may wish to have include:

1 A class list of the children with their dates of birth and the results of any standardised tests. A list of children with specific problems is also very useful.

2 Examples of the school's text books — especially Maths, English and Science.

3 Any record sheets for the children.

4 An account of the work the children covered last year.

5 A record book.

6 The school's Curriculum Policy document. (That should panic the Headteacher!)

7 A plan of the school. (Maybe in Handbook)

8 A list of the television and radio programmes the previous teacher ordered.

9 A timetable.

10 Price of staffroom coffee.

You will also need to know where you can park your car, where your pigeon hole is located, where you can hang your coat and where you can sit in the staffroom.

The Survival Kit

These are some resources that most teachers would say were indispensable but we never think of until we actually need them!

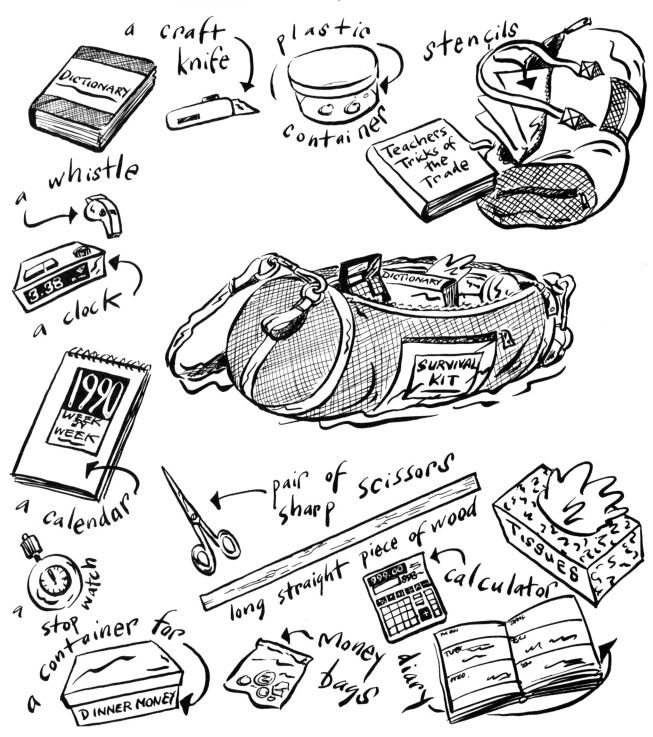

a craft knife

plastic container

stencils

DICTIONARY

Teachers Tricks of the Trade

a whistle

a clock 3.38

1990 WEEK BY WEEK

SURVIVAL KIT

DICTIONARY

a calendar

pair of sharp scissors

Tissues

long straight piece of wood

999.00 calculator

a stop watch

a container for DINNER MONEY

Money bags

diary

and, lastly, something which no teacher can be without — a sense of humour

Classroom Organisation

Equipment

Ideally you should have:

1 Enough desks and tables of the correct size for the children. This is important as class sizes change from year to year. Watch out for the extra large/small child who may need a different sized table to the rest of the class. Any spare tables can be used for display.

2 A teacher's desk/table and chair of adult size.

3 Tray units if the children use tables.

4 Some form of storage.

5 A sink — if you haven't don't despair, there are ways round this. Make an arrangement with a more fortunate colleague that you may use her sink for any activities needing water and a small number of children. Try to get hold of a large polybin beer container (empty!) or large squash containers to hold any fresh water you made need. (However you must impress on the children that the water must **never** be drunk). For art lessons have several buckets for: fresh water (or for catching drips while they decant fresh water), old mixing water and dirty brushes and palettes. Trusted monitors can carry the buckets to wherever they can wash up.

   If you particularly want an item you cannot beg, borrow or swipe from another classroom try contacting your Local Education Office. They often have a pool of unwanted furniture which they will be only too happy to let you have. I got three teacher's desks, two storage units for the staffroom and a piano that way in one term!

You will also need:

▷ Newspaper

▷ Scissors

▷ Paints and brushes

▷ Palettes — mixing and paint if you are lucky

▷ Water containers

▷ Fabric scraps

▷ Clock

▷ Chalkboard rubber

▷ Staple gun and staples

▷ Staple extractor

▷ Stapler and staples

▷ Craft knife (or rotatrim if you are very lucky!)

▷ Chalkboard ruler (with perhaps compass and setsquare)

Most schools have this equipment in every classroom. If you arrive and find that you are a staple gun short, ask. It has been known for the equipment of one teacher to be acquired by others when she leaves and not left in the room for the incoming teacher.

Arrangement of furniture

The arrangement of your classroom is usually left to your personal preference. There are two main ways.

▷ **Lines:** This is very formal but it is much easier to keep the children under control as they only have one person they can talk to. It is less distracting for them and they are all facing the front so they can see the chalkboard clearly. However, for any group work and, possibly, art and craft you will have to have a major furniture shuffle which can undo all the good discipline instilled by the rows in the first place!

▷ **Groups:** This is obviously less formal. The children can communicate with the rest of the group which may be excellent for their oral skills but not for your discipline. It is easier for the children to share items such as a pot of coloured pencils. Groups of tables also seem to take up less space so you can have areas in your classroom for display, art etc.

Try to have a spare desk/cushion/chair for children to go to when they are not behaving as you would wish. Some teachers use this system as a punishment, isolating the child so that he does his work properly and doesn't disturb others. Others use it as a private place where child (and teacher) can go and sit and not be disturbed until they feel they can cope with the stresses of the classroom again or until an angry and upset child (or teacher) has calmed down.

Some infant and temporary classrooms have clothes pegs in the classroom. When labelling their pegs think about how you are going to dismiss them. (It is never a good idea to let the whole class go at once.) If you dismiss them in groups, don't put the whole group of children together. Leave spare pegs at regular intervals to give the children more space. Some infant teachers label their children's pegs with a colour or symbol until the child can recognise his name. The same colour/symbol is then used on his tray, books etc.

Storage

Unless you are exceptionally lucky, you will never have enough storage space. Ways round this are to acquire more cupboards (see *Equipment*) or to make the very best use of what you have. An idea to increase your storage space is to cover your spare tables with a large piece of fabric (an old curtain is ideal), use the top for display and store items in boxes underneath, hidden by the fabric.

Other ideas for storage

▷ Old plastic bread baskets are ideal for PE equipment and lunch-boxes.

▷ E5 Washing powder boxes, covered, are just the right size for storing magazines, workcards and anything of A4 size.

▷ Biscuit tins, solid emulsion containers are the right size for storing paper.

▷ 450g tins are useful for powder paint, coloured pencils, felt-tips etc.

▷ Large petfood tins are ideal for group pencils and rulers, paintbrushes etc.

▷ Old liquid soap containers are useful for decanted paint as the children find it easier to get paint out of them with the plunging action.

▷ Any small jars or containers are useful for storing glue.

▷ Margarine containers are wonderful for anything small such as needles, threads, buttons, clay tools, nibs, dinner money etc.

▷ Fruit boxes are ideal for anything A4 laid on its side. I have three containing all my worksheets. I have used the cardboard covers from old exercise books as dividers.

▷ Large tins, e.g. coffee, are useful for musical instrument beaters, spare rulers etc.

▷ Plastic egg-boxes can be used as paint palettes.

▷ Record storage boxes (LP's) can be used for overhead projector sheets.

▷ Ice-cream containers are wonderful for anything else too bulky to go into margarine containers.

Organising equipment

The key to organising equipment in the classroom is to have everything in a labelled container (for children who can't read you can use a drawing of the item) in a special place. This may be a box, tin, tray, shelf of a cupboard, but if it is labelled then everyone knows where it goes and you can see at a glance what is missing. This applies especially to items like scissors which mysteriously disappear no matter how strict you are about counting them in or out. The only fool-proof way I know of keeping all my scissors for the whole year is to colour code them by putting coloured sticky tape round the handle and keeping them in a storage container like the one shown. At the end of the day when the scissors are checked one can see at a glance how many pairs are missing.

As well as colour coding scissors, I colour code, or label with my class number, all the items of equipment that belong to my classroom. In this way I know that I will get my staple-gun back when it has been borrowed.

A way of organising those awkward pieces of maths equipment needed for the maths scheme which 'only uses pieces of equipment found in every primary classroom' (since when was the *AA Book of the Road* found in every primary classroom?) is to put each one in a labelled plastic bag and attach it to the wall by a bulldog clip. Label the wall behind the bag so that you know what is missing. This is particularly good for equipment such as: 'two red counters', 'a metre piece of string' or '15cm of 5mm dowelling' (I never did find out what that was used for). To find the list of equipment needed by your maths/science scheme try looking in the front/back of the teacher's book. It's usually listed and incredibly useful.

Nowadays many schools use a colour coding system for organising their reading books (see *Organising Reading*), but books which you will have to be responsible for are topic books. For years I returned my topic boxes one or two books short until a colleague showed me his idea of tying coloured wool around the spine so that the books were readily identifiable and didn't disappear into trays or the library unnoticed.

Keeping the classroom tidy

1 Have a place for everything, and make sure everyone knows where that place is.

2 Have monitors to look after certain pieces of equipment e.g. scissors, the box of newspapers.

3 Give each group of children a section of the class that is their responsibility. Make it a competition to see who keeps their area of the classroom tidiest.

4 Insist upon tidiness and respect for other people's property. Lay down your standards and make sure they stick to them. Give them at least ten minutes at the end of a session to tidy up, then point out what is wrong. Reward the helpful and punish the vandal — hard. If there is no obvious culprit forbid the whole class use of the item and withdraw it from temptation.

5 Make it **very** clear exactly what they may and may not use during a wet playtime. Make sure the dinner ladies know this as well.

Children's equipment

The children's equipment should be kept in their labelled trays/desks. The only way to make sure the labelling of trays will survive the year is to cover the label with sticky-backed plastic. Cut out the plastic about 2cm bigger than the label. Stick the label in the middle and then use the extra sticky-backed plastic round the sides to stick it to the tray. If you cover the label and use glue or sellotape to stick it to the tray it will fall off within a term — guaranteed.

They will also need a pencil and a ruler. Label them both if you can. Pencils are best labelled with their name on a piece of paper stuck on with sellotape. You can label them by cutting a sliver of wood off the end of the pencil and writing the name in felt-tip onto the pencil. However, this has two disadvantages: a child that chews the end of his pencil gets a black mouth and an illegibly named pencil and the name wears off/becomes too grubby to read in a very short time. I allow a new pencil every half term. Some children require more, some less, but do not give out a new pencil simply because the child can't find his own or you will go through several thousand a year.

If a child genuinely needs his pencil replaced frequently, try giving him an H or a 2H pencil. It could be that he presses too hard and is having to sharpen his pencil too frequently. This also applies to the child who never seems to have a sharp pencil despite your wrath and reminders.

Rulers are inevitably handed on from one year to the next. A good scrub at the end of the year freshens them up, especially if they are plastic. Remember that the child has to use the ruler so don't make the label so large that it covers up the numbers along the edge!

11

Rubbers are a real problem. For some reason children love to eat them. Heaven only knows why but if they don't disappear completely, then they will have strange tooth marks on them. The moral with rubbers is the more you give out the more you will lose. Husband them jealously. I used to have one super-large rubber tied to my desk by a piece of string. The children could use it whenever they needed. An alternative is to give each group a large rubber, labelled with the name/initial/number of the group, termly.

Pencil sharpeners are also a problem. The large electric type are best for infants as their small hands cannot manage any other. The large mechanical ones keep going wrong and the small ones need a certain amount of finesse unless you are going to break the lead every time and end up sharpening the pencil down to nothing. Pencil sharpeners should be freely available at all times. Some teachers have monitors to sharpen the pencils daily.

Classroom areas

Most modern primary classrooms are divided into 'areas', for maths, English, art/craft and reading with perhaps a topic or a display area. How you use these areas is up to you. Some teachers have the activity only going on in that area. Some use that area only for storage or display. Room dividers can consist of furniture such as bookshelves or tables or tray units with display boarding or large sheets of corrugated cardboard. If you have displays suitable only for the subject matter of that area it helps give you the self-discipline to have displays covering the whole area of the curriculum and not just your main subject.

All the equipment must be readily available for the children. Label everything. Don't stack things or put things on high shelves or at the back of a table. Remember they are smaller than you!

Display

All too often a teacher is considered 'good' by the quality of her displays. We know this in our heart of hearts so we slave over them after school. We try to think of new and original ideas. Yes, we do need to make our classrooms an attractive environment for children but first a few words of warning. Children very rarely take any notice of any display once it has gone up. Very few of them will bother to read your well-thought-out headings and explanations. Most of them will only look for their own work. Children have no sense of quality and will be quite happy to have any old rubbish on the wall as long as it has their name on it and you tell their Mum.

So let us get displays into perspective: unless you are very careful you spend hours creating a beautiful classroom to impress visitors, but with very little educational value to the children.

A few golden rules

1 Displays must be changed frequently. Children only really look at them when they are first put up. Change at least one of your displays a week to keep things fresh. This may mean that the quality of the display may not be as good as if you changed them termly, but it is the children that count.

2 Have some trick to get the children to **look** at the display. Offer a reward to the first person to

▷ answer a question posed by the display;
▷ add something to the display;
▷ use a new word taught by the display;
▷ perform a task asked for by the display.

3 Have different types of display

▷ **Information:** This includes pictures, diagrams and text which supplement what you are trying to teach the children or the results of the children's findings e.g. in topic work. Giving each group of children part of a display to complete is very rewarding, but requires good organisation and you, at least, must know exactly what you are aiming for in the finished article.

▷ **Interactive:** With this type of display the children participate in some way e.g. filling in words on a spiders web of words, putting a poem on the poetry tree, writing down words they've found with this week's sound in, etc.

▷ **Displaying good work:** All children love having their work on the wall. Display only the best work of each child (standards will, of course, vary). If writing the piece out again is a chore, use the computer. Here we are aiming for quality (and, hopefully legibility!). Try to have at least one display with a piece of work from each child.

Any of the above can be two or three dimensional.

Mounting the Work

Although for speed you can put the work directly onto the background, it is worth the extra effort of mounting it (especially if you can train the children or a helpful mum or dad to do it).

Hints for mounting work

1 Double mounting is the best but it is time and paper consuming. An idea to save paper is to cut out strips of paper of the secondary colour and stick them around the edge of the mounted work.

2 Mounting work and then drawing a line about 5mm from the edge of the work gives an appearance of double mounting.

3 Try mounting several pieces of work at different angles on a larger sheet of paper.

4 Mount the work on a piece of paper with an appropriate shape e.g. leaves for autumn, cars for transport.

Making effective displays

Backgrounds

▷ **Fabric:**   This is very effective, especially if draped. Scour jumble sales for old sheets, duvet covers or curtains.

▷ **Hessian:**   This looks alright and lasts a long time.

▷ **Sugar paper:**   Choose a colour to co-ordinate with the mounting paper. It will fade, Blu-tack rips it and it will have to be replaced with each new display. However it can be used in a variety of ways.

▷ **Gummed paper:**   In large sheets this has the advantage over sugar paper in that the colours are bright, Blu-tack will peel off it (with care) so that it can last for repeated displays. This hopefully, will out-weigh its increased cost.

▷ **Proprietary backing paper:**   This is expensive, but excellent. Bright colours, will usually last a whole year (or more). Blu-tack peels off easily.

▷ **Unusual ideas to fit the display:**   Try newspaper, marbled/stippled/spray diffused paper, a large painting, pictures from catalogues/magazines, leaf/potato/rag-rolled prints.

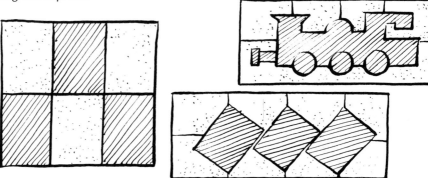

5   When mounting large pieces of art work which will not fit onto a piece of mounting paper, cut the paper into strips and stick the strips onto the front of the work to make a mock window mount.

6   When giving the children art paper (i.e. A2 paper cut into half or quarters) make the children leave a border of about 2cm. When you come to mount the work, trim this off and the work will then fit onto A2 paper for mounting easily.

7   Children's writing looks better on plain rather than lined paper. Make them some line guides by going over lined paper in black felt-tip and mounting them on card. This then goes underneath the plain paper the child is writing on. If you leave a border on the line guide there will be a border on the finished work.

8   Borders are always effective. An easy way to get the children to make a border is to get them to leave a narrow ruler's width round the edge of the paper and then to decorate it.

9   When using a stapler, angle the staples so that they are not flat into the board. They will then be more easily removed by a staple extractor.

Titles and borders

1   Stencils look wonderful, but are time consuming. If you think that they are neat enough try to get the children to draw round the letters.

2   Try to make the lettering fit the subject of the display (very impressive) e.g.

3   Draw pictures around the edge of the letters appropriate to the subject of the display.

4   Mount your title and cover with sticky-backed plastic. After all your work you don't want to throw it away and then you can use it another time (when you change schools!).

5   Borders look fantastic but take hours to do. Get the children to make them by drawing a picture or a length of pattern each.

One last word about displays. If you do them properly, cover them and keep them (in a large, labelled folder) you will always be able to use them again. It's amazing how versatile some display material is. It is time consuming the first time you do it but as you take it out of the folder at the beginning of term you will be very thankful that you took the trouble.

Beginning the year

You will need to go in at least a day early to sort out your classroom. Here is a list of some of the things you will need to do:

1 Organise the furniture.

2 Put up backing paper/displays.

3 Have the children's books and equipment ready.

4 Have your stock ready.

5 Prepare anything you may need for the children e.g. record folders, reading book markers.

6 Label trays, clothes pegs and books. (If you label your books always in the same order, and use the same order for your trays it is then extremely simple to post the books into the trays — so simple that your old class can do it. It is also easy to see when you have forgotten to write out a particular book for a child.)

7 Write out your registers.

8 Find out if there are any special medical needs in your new class.

9 Sign up your class on any rotas e.g. computer, TV.

10 Fill glue containers

11 If you wish your children to sit in a certain place, put their tray/books on top of their table/desk and ask them to sit where they find their name.

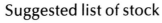

Suggested list of stock

For the teacher	For the children
record book	exercise books
mark book	pencils
red pens	rulers
black pens	rubbers
chalk	felt-tips
register	colouring pencils
dinner register	paints
staples	glue and spreaders
large felt-tips	plain paper
Blu-tak	lined paper
drawing pins	tracing paper
	scissors

If you are new to the school you will also need to know:

1 Your way around the school.

2 The school times.

3 Where the stock is kept and arrangements for getting some.

4 Staff list.

5 Arrangements for playground duty.

6 Arrangements for using the TV and computer.

7 Where the reading books are kept.

8 How the children are dismissed from school.

9 The arrangements for play-time coffee.

Hopefully your new school will have a School Handbook. Most schools do. Ask about one, it's possible someone has forgotten to give it to you.

Don't forget to bring in a mug for your play-time drinks. Most of the spare cups found in a staff room are used for unmentionable purposes in art lessons.

The end of the year

Despite the euphoria engendered by six weeks of freedom, the end of the year is even harder work than the beginning.

Things to be done at the end of the year:

1 Clear out all cupboards, bookcases, boxes etc. and throw away all rubbish.

2 Take down all displays, give work back to children.

3 Wipe over reading books (it's amazing the difference it makes).

4 Tidy up all books, workcards, equipment.

5 Clean all plastic equipment.

6 Clean rulers and children's trays.

7 Empty children's trays. To do this I find the following easiest. The night before, insist that they take home all personal possessions. Get them to put their trays out onto their tables. All unused exercised books to be returned to you. All covers of remaining exercise books to be pulled off whole. These are usually made of card and can be used in a variety of ways over the next year. All spare pages out of half-used exercise books to be carefully torn out and put on a pile in a central place. This paper, once trimmed, can be used instead of file paper or as scrap, depending on how good your children are at tearing out the pages. All rubbish to go into a bin liner. Do not let them screw up paper. You will get much more in the liner if the paper is flat.

8 Get as ready as you can for next year.

Planning

So here you are, looking at your immaculately laid out classroom, alive with display, children all grouped nicely, pencils and rulers named, but what will you do with them for five hours a day, five days a week for the next eleven months? The key to the problem is planning. You have to know where you (and the children) are going and then sort out how you are going to get there. So let's take things a step at a time:

Planning the year

Your main structure will be provided by the National Curriculum. You will know from the folders available in all schools the programme of work you will be expected to cover for your children. The National Curriculum was not intended to be the sole aim of teachers and hopefully most teachers will incorporate the tasks necessary to fulfil the requirements of the National Curriculum within the type of work already done.

To plan your year's work you will need to know exactly what your children have covered before they came into your class. The structure of the National Curriculum has advantages because you will know from the previous teacher which attainment targets have been met. You will be able to incorporate building upon these skills and experiences in your own long-term planning for the year.

By the end of the Summer Holidays you should have some idea of what your topics are going to be and what you are going to cover in the main areas of the curriculum.

In the *Appendices* on p144–147 you will find diagrams of the main skills for some subject areas. You may find these helpful when preparing your aims.

Planning the Timetable

No matter which method of teaching you prefer you will need to know what you expect your children to cover by the end of each week. Here is a list of the main activities found in a primary classroom which may help you to plan the activities for your children.

▷ **Mathematics**   arithmetic
practical
investigative
mental

▷ **Language**   grammar
                     punctuation
                     writing — creative, descriptive, poetic, informative
                     spelling
                     oral

▷ **Reading**   silent reading
                     games and activities
                     phonics
                     group reading
                     class story
                     reading aloud
                     cloze
                     comprehension

▷ **Handwriting**

▷ **RE**

▷ **Science**

▷ **Computer**

▷ **History**

▷ **Geography**

▷ **Drama**

▷ **Gymnastics**

▷ **Games**

▷ **Dance**

▷ **Music**

▷ **Art and Craft**

▷ **Topic**

with perhaps:

▷ **Television programmes**

▷ **Radio programmes**

▷ **Swimming**

A lot to cover in twenty-five hours!

The easiest way to make sure that all the activities you have decided to be necessary are done is to have a particular time for every child to do them each week — a timetable. This can be the same for the whole class (needs more resources, is very wearing if they all need help at the same time, but at least you only have to teach the lesson once), different for each child (requires a large amount of planning and highly organised record keeping but does cater exactly for the individual needs of every child) or a timetable for groups of children (needs fewer resources, but the lesson can pall by the time you get to the last group).

Another method is to allocate a rough time you would expect each child to spend on each necessary activity e.g.

Half an hour	One hour	One hour +
Handwriting	Science	Mathematics
RE	Topic	Art/craft
Group Reading	Reading Activities	
Spelling Activities	Creative Writing	
Drama	Games	
Gymnastics		
Television		
Music		
Language development		
Storytime		
History		
Geography		

Put onto your timetable the subjects which cannot be changed e.g. Games and Hall times. Next, block in the rest of the activities according to your children or groups.

To introduce the work to the children sometimes you can say 'I would like this . . . this . . . and this finished by the end of the morning. I don't mind which order you do them in.' This helps children to discipline themselves and learn to pace themselves. Often children will operate their own reward system and do something they enjoy after something they dislike. In my class they only leave the work they dislike to the end, and then say they didn't have time, once.

Grouping children

Many teachers group children for a variety of reasons:
    it helps their language development
    it fosters social skills
    it's convenient

Basically they can be grouped in 5 ways:
    by the same age
    by deliberately mixing ages (vertical grouping)
    by the same ability

by mixing abilities
by friendship

Children might be in different groups according to the lesson e.g. an ability group for spelling, a friendship group for art and a vertical group for drama.

Individual Planning

In order to plan for the continued development of each child in all areas of the curriculum you will have to be aware of the ground they have already covered. This may be in the form of records from the previous teacher, your own knowledge of the child or from the results of tests — your own or standardised. The problem with records is that to a great extent they are subjective and we all know that there is a world of difference between the class having 'done' question marks and little Johnny actually knowing when and how to use them in his own writing. The standardised tests are usually a good guide as long as you are aware of their limitations. Your own tests at the beginning of the year are usually very useful. You can then take the results of these tests and plan your lessons to fill in gaps in the child's skills and to build on existing knowledge. For further details on making your own tests please look at the chapter on *Record Keeping and Testing*.

Making full use of all resources

To help you in your teaching you will need supplementary material. It must be very boring for children to have to listen to one person all the time, however gifted a teacher they may be. To this end try to make full use of all available resources so that teaching is not all 'chalk and talk' and the children are learning from a variety of stimuli.

The main resources at your disposal are:

Your Local Authority Resources

Most LEAs have resources available to teachers — these may take the form of:

A Teachers' Centre

These may have some Maths equipment, copying facilities, teachers' handbooks, copies of radio and TV booklets and programmes and the knowledge of where to go for help if you have a specific problem.

The Teachers' Resource Centre

This may be part of the Library Service. They may have fiction and non-fiction books with perhaps the facility for Topic Boxes (boxes of books and resources on a specific subject to be borrowed for the duration of your topic, usually termly or half-termly); teachers reference books; visual aids such as display posters etc. and usually a wealth of information on local history and geography, including Ordnance Survey maps.

A Teachers' Loan Service

Some LEAs operate a teachers' loan service for large items which might be useful aids such as complete or part skeletons, stuffed animals and birds, examples of natural phenomena e.g. wasps or ants nests. There may be a book which lists these items somewhere in your school.

Audio-Visual Aids Service

Many Authorities operate a loan system for films, filmstrips, slides, videos and even computer software which teachers can borrow. Usually there is a catalogue of what is available in schools and other establishments. You do have to be very organised to order these though, as they often require the order up to three weeks before you need the article. However, they may deliver to the school, if you are lucky!

The Inspectorate

Many Inspectors/Advisors have their own departments with equipment which teachers may borrow. The idea is for teachers to try out a piece of expensive equipment in the classroom before actually buying it in case it is not suitable. This particularly applies to Maths and Science which may have their own Resource Centres.

TV and Radio Programmes

Both television companies provide a wide range of programmes to suit all ages and abilities. Their information booklet usually arrives at the school in the late spring and the orders for books etc. have to be posted by sometime in May. If you arrive at a school in September and you are desperate for the Teachers' Book for a certain programme you can write to, or telephone, the address given in the booklet.

Large Companies and Organisations

If your work for the next year covers areas such as communications, conservation, energy, manufacturing, foodstuffs etc. try writing (or getting the children to write) to the major company concerned for any resources they may provide. A list of such companies and organisations is provided in a book called *Free Stuff For Kids* (Exley Publications) which is very useful.

Places of Interest

Often Museums and places of interest will provide you with information relevant to your topic, especially if you decide to take the children there on a day visit.

Planning the Lessons

Having decided what the children are going to achieve by the end of a certain period of time (for the purpose of this book we are going to take a week at a time which is what many teachers use) you now have to decide how the children are going to do the tasks i.e. plan your lesson. Lesson planning is a much undervalued part of the teacher's job. Most children (and some parents!) believe that the teacher comes into the classroom and things just happen. But before that happens most teachers will have spent some time planning their lesson. The time taken on planning varies tremendously with the type of lesson and age and experience of both children and teacher. But lessons do have to be planned if they are not to be one-off-occupy-a-child-times. Most teachers write down their lesson plans in a book. Some do it by subject and others by day but this record is a very useful reminder of what you have done with the children and what worked and what was not quite so successful. Some Headteachers ask to see these books regularly — you have been warned!

When planning lessons it is helpful to start with what exactly you want the child to have learned from the lesson — remember this does not always have to be factual; you may wish to build up his confidence or get him to sit still for ten minutes. Try to be as precise as possible. For example, if you want the child to learn about capital letters, do you mean just at the beginning of sentences or at the beginning of proper nouns and when speech marks are opened as well. Well obviously only the former I hear you mutter, after all he is only eight. Fine — but does he have an understanding of what a sentence is and are you going to teach full stops at the same time?

Having decided upon your subject matter you then need to decide how you are going to introduce it ('Turn to Book Four, page two,' is not really the most exciting way of introducing anything — but useful if you're feeling fragile). The idea is to get them interested and to get over the teaching point you wish to make. After the introduction comes the work you want the child to do to re-inforce what it is you wish him to learn. Most teachers will have some idea how long this should take. Infants will whizz through everything like greased lightning, lower juniors will take forever if you let them and upper juniors will work at length if they are interested and at a reasonable speed if they are not (gross generalisations, I know). Even experienced teachers make mistakes as to the length of time a task may take. A way of checking to see if it is you or them is to see how many have finished by the time set. If over half of them are still hard at work then you have probably miscalculated. Praise them for their hard work and re-set your deadline.

More experienced teachers will often simply note the subject of the lesson in their records, but they will still have a clear idea of how they are going to teach the lesson. When you have taught capital letters for the five-thousandth time you don't feel the need to write these things down. Newer teachers may feel more secure if they have a more precise lesson plan and students often need to provide an evaluation.

Please remember that lessons are about the children and not the subject. 'Set lessons' do not usually work because each child/group of children is different and a lesson which is very successful with one child/group may flop with another. This is one of the reasons why teaching is such hard work. You have to be aware of your children and adapt your lessons to their particular needs.

Having planned your week's lessons it is highly improbable the class will achieve half of what you have planned and you will almost certainly have to swap lessons round or even change your lesson completely to take advantage of the only sunny afternoon that week/some exciting event/the dental inspection which you clean forgot about. The end of the Christmas term is infamous for this.

Parents, Welfare Assistants and Other Organisations

Parents

Most educationalists would see a child's education as being a partnership between parents and school. How much this partnership is developed and explored will depend on the policy of your Headteacher. Many schools welcome parents informally into the playground and classroom, some schools will insist parents stop at the school gate and venture onto school property only when attending an official appointment.

When seeing parents try to remember the following:

1 They may be quite nervous about seeing you. Try to put them at their ease i.e. say that you are pleased to see them. This really puts them off their stroke if they've come to complain!

2 The parents may have a different view of the child from you. This view may not necessarily be wrong. Children react differently in different circumstances and the quiet little soul at the back of your class may be a loud-mouthed little monster at home.

3 Be truthful, but tactful. If the child is badly behaved or has learning difficulties, tell them, but stress any good points such as the child is good at sport or tries extremely hard. Don't over-emphasise small problems. Parents will often remember what you say out of context and may be very concerned about something which you regarded as trivial but told them because you could think of nothing else of note to say about the child.

4 Try not to use educational jargon when dealing with parents. It may sound good to you but will only antagonise them or worry them further.

5 Make a note of anything important which came up at the interview and also of any action which you agreed to take. The former may be serious enough to go on the child's record and it's very easy to forget the latter after your twenty-fifth parent.

Parents' Evenings

In a formal situation these may be the only opportunities parents have of meeting you and seeing the place where their child spends most of his day. However, such occasions have two main problems. In a primary school each interview may only last between five and ten minutes and other parents may be in the room, able to overhear what you have to say. Also, you will probably not see the parents that you most wish to see.

Parents' Evenings are not really the time to discuss any serious matters because of the reasons already given. If you have something serious to discuss with the parents arrange a separate interview at a later date. Parents' Evenings are really only suitable for concerned parents to see their child's work, meet you and ascertain that all is well.

When a Parents' Evening is planned, a letter will go home asking the parents to indicate which teacher(s) they would like to see and which times (usually within a half-hour band) would be most convenient. When you have all your slips, it is a nice gesture to liaise with teachers of other classes so that children from the same family do not have widely differing appointments. Write out your appointment times on a large sheet of paper and fill in the names of the parents so that most of them are near their requested times. It is helpful to leave some gaps in your list to allow for any parents who run over their time and to give yourself a break. To help keep to time some teachers display this list, others keep an alarm clock on their desk or set their watch to 'peep' at ten minute intervals. Unfortunately Parents' Evenings are rather like doctors' surgeries, if one set of parents over-run their time, even if the next set of parents have no problems at all they will insist upon their full length of time.

To help to pass the time while they are waiting, parents like to look at their child's work. (It can be heartstopping as they flick past your acerbic comments and you may wish you hadn't written 'rubbish' across that awful story last Tuesday.) It looks neater if the children put their books out tidily on their desks. If you ask them to get out their trays be prepared for a mammoth clear out of old sweetpapers and toys. Although you may find out where the missing topic books have disappeared to.

Another idea for Parents' Evening is for the children to write a letter to their parents asking them to look specifically at certain pieces of their work on display. e.g. 'Please look at my Teddy Bear poem on the blue notice board.'

Parents' Evenings can also be useful times to sell items to parents such as uniform, pamphlets, the school magazine, books, etc.

In a large school you may have to give parents a plan of the school or leave a large plan in a prominent position such as the lobby or hall.

Disgruntled Parents

You may have cause to deal with a parent who is far from happy. This is not a pleasant situation and whether you are in the right or in the wrong it is better for all concerned if you can part amicably. If you find yourself confronted with angry parents here are some helpful ideas:

1 Keep them waiting for a few minutes while you deal with an emergency/ telephone call/go and get help. If the anger is impulsive a few minutes respite may calm the situation down.

2 Greet the parents politely and say how pleased you are to see them. Show them that you are just as eager as they are to sort out this difficult situation with their child.

3 Ask them to tell you what is wrong. You will then have a clear idea of what you are defending yourself against. Often the parent has believed the child's interpretation of an event which may have been misrepresented through

deliberate falsehood or immaturity. Explain clearly your understanding of the situation. Try not to blame the child (unless there has been some obviously deliberate blatant lying) but interpret events kindly. In this way everyone saves face, especially the parent for believing the child in the first place. Most parents will accept your explanation of events and together you can then proceed to sort out the problem. However, there are some parents who will never believe that their child could be mistaken and may become abusive. In this event you would be advised to seek the help of your Headteacher. If you know you have a difficult interview with parents coming up it is wise to let your Head know. Many Headteachers would prefer to deal with this kind of situation personally, anyway. If you are truly on your own it may be wise to suggest to the parent that you will look into the matter further and make an appointment for another time when help is at hand or you can get the evidence you need. If all else fails you will have to respectfully suggest to the parents that you will have to settle for a difference of opinion but you will bear their wishes in mind in future dealings with their child.

Try not to get too upset after an unpleasant interview. For every parent who would like to do unmentionable things to your person, there are many more who are very grateful for all you have done for their child. It is very easy to become despondent after such an interview and to lose your self-confidence. If you feel this way, take a look at some of the successes you have had and some of the positive things that have happened and put it all down to experience.

Open Days/Evenings

These differ from Parents' Evenings in that there is no formal timetable. Parents and friends are invited into the school while the children are working to see what happens in school. Most parents are intrigued by what happens in a modern primary school and like to come in and see the books and equipment that their child is so excited about.

Some schools may put on special displays for parents to watch e.g. gymnastics or drama. In the evening these will guarantee that at least some parents will come.

It is not really wise to do anything special for an Open Day. A tidy classroom and foolproof lessons are the best idea. If you do something unusual the parents will know because their offspring will tell them and then it won't be a typical school day.

Parents of Pre-school Children

The policy of liaising with the parents of pre-school children will depend on your Headteacher and will vary enormously from school to school. Some schools offer a great deal of help and advice to parents and may even loan equipment and books. Some schools hold evenings to introduce parents to the school. The children usually come for some introductory mornings/afternoons or days before they start full-time education, but this will depend on your LEA and Headteacher.

As a reception infant teacher your role in introducing children to school life cannot be over-estimated and a part of that task is dealing with parents who may not have been parted from their children before.

Here are some hints which may prove helpful:

1 Try to meet the parent(s) before the child's first day at school. Then they will not regard the teacher as a complete stranger and this may reduce their anxiety.

2 Try to have activities ready in which the children can become immediately involved. This will help the child take his mind off the parents and they in turn will be reassured that the child is able to cope without them.

3 Let the parents help the child prepare for the school day and then encourage them to leave.

4 A crying child is best cuddled by the teacher, and the parents encouraged to leave. Explain that they have things to do but they will be back at the end of school. Try to find a special job for the child to do to 'help' you. Have soft toys available for the child to cuddle or a puppet who is also starting his first day at school.

5 A very distressed child may need a security corner. A soft cushion or place where he can go and cuddle a soft toy and sleep if he cannot cope and needs time to adjust.

Parents as Helpers

Some schools or PTA's have a list of parents with useful skills who would be prepared to lend their time to help the school, for example in painting or keeping livestock. Some parents are prepared to help in the classroom on a regular basis and their help can be extremely valuable.

If a parent (usually a Mum) offers to help you in your classroom, ask them if they have any preference as to the kind of help they would like to offer. If they are polite and leave the decision to you, ask them if they have any particular hobbies or skills which they would like to help the children with. In this way you may be able to set up a machine sewing group, or pottery group, or a cookery group. Although they probably have considerable expertise in their chosen skill, they will need your help to organise what exactly they have to do. For example the machine embroiderer may not realise that the children will have to be taught to thread the machine, machine in a straight line, practise stopping and starting, practise the zig-zag technique and how to finish off. These stages will have to be gone through before their first simple designs can be attempted.

Any parent in the classroom will have to know your ground rules for acceptable behaviour so that they can insist upon your own high standards! This is especially important if they are listening to children reading. Whatever your record keeping system or arrangements for changing books, the parent must be made aware of this so that the children do not become confused.

Parents usually offer their help in school because they enjoy working with the children. Most Mums and Dads would prefer to help a group of children rather than wash up paint pots every afternoon. However, if you can get a dedicated parent into your classroom they will be worth their weight in gold. They will be able to do all the things that you would like to be able to do if you were not so tired and hard-pressed trying to cover all areas of the curriculum by the end of the year.

Some teachers find another adult in their classroom threatening. If you do not know the parent personally, it can be a nerve-racking experience for the first few weeks. But remember that the parent will feel insecure as well in an alien environment over which they have no control. Your first task is to make them feel at ease and to build a working relationship with them. Once this is done you will have no need to feel threatened. Very, very rarely the parent will come into the classroom as a 'spy' to make sure that their child is being taught as they would wish. You may hear of their disapproval through third parties. If you are feeling brave, or self-righteous, you may wish to 'discuss' your differences with them. But a safer move is to 'lend' them to another class who are desperate for help to make their crib/costumes/masks.

Other Organisations

As a teacher you will be concerned with the whole child and not just his academic skills. Teachers play a very important role in the lives of children and most of us can remember certain teachers who have influenced us at one time or another.

Often a teacher may discover something about a child that his family were unaware of. Children may even trust their teacher more than their parents. This is a very heavy responsibility which can be very rewarding or extremely frustrating as you have no legal rights over the child once he leaves the school premises.

Because of our very special relationship with children we are often in a privileged position to notice when anything may be seriously wrong with the child. This may be physical or emotional. If you suspect there might be a serious problem in the child's life, it is a good idea to begin to keep a record. You may then notice that the child is sullen and withdrawn only when Daddy is home or is ravenously hungry on Mondays. Another area which may indicate that the child is undergoing some form of abuse is in his expressive activities such as play, drama, mime, family drawings and 'news'.

Things to look out for which may indicate that a child is being abused include:

1 A fearful or cowering attitude towards adults.

2 Unexplained injuries.

3 Serious injuries where the explanation is unlikely.

4 Serious injuries where medical attention is not sought.

5 Frequent absences from school.

6 Problems with eating and sleeping.

7 The child may be very withdrawn.

8 Bleeding, soreness or discharge from genital or rectal areas.

If you notice signs such as these which could be interpreted as physical abuse, get a second opinion from someone in authority that day. Never let the child know your suspicions (unless they have come to you of their own accord to confide in you). Commiserate privately and give the child an opportunity to explain. If you are still suspicious do not give the child the benefit of the doubt. Children have a strong sense of loyalty towards their parents and in cases of abuse this could be strengthened by fear. You can always think up some reason for consulting another teacher about the bruise or burns under the assumed guise of your lack of knowledge in first-aid.

We all aim to foster an atmosphere in our classroom where children feel free to express themselves and grow to trust themselves, their peers and their teacher. The classroom may be a place where the child feels secure and he may wish to disclose to his teacher problems that are troubling him. If a child confides in you try to remember the following:

1 The child has confided in you because he trusts you. Do not immediately go and fetch other colleagues to listen to the child as well.

2 Show the child that you believe what he is saying no matter how bizarre the statement.

3 Try not to react to anything the child may say, but remain compassionate and sympathetic according to circumstances. Try not to express opinions, just listen.

4 After the child has finished sharing his experiences try to recapitulate with the child what he has just told you. You are obviously unable to take notes in this situation so it is important that an often mixed up account is clarified in your own mind before further action is taken.

5 After the child has shared his problems with you he may be frightened at the unknown consequences of his actions. Emphasise to the child that he has done the right thing in telling you.

6 Realise that when the child becomes aware of the importance to adults of the information he has imparted he may then deny the validity of his statement.

If you have evidence or strong suspicions that all is not well with the child at home, inform your Headteacher immediately. He will have set procedures to follow and may call in one of the following services for help to deal with the problem.

The Educational Welfare Service

These officers have come a long way from their old role as School Attendance Officers. They are now consulted if there is any doubt about the care of the child at home. They liaise with the other agencies a great deal and are very useful allies.

The School Psychological Service

If a child is not making progress or has behavioural or emotional difficulties you may ask for him to be tested by an Educational Psychologist. Depending on the nature of the problem, the Educational Psychologist will test the child and may be able to recommend either a programme which may help the child or that the child should be referred to another agency. An Educational Psychologist's report is necessary for statementing a child.

Child Guidance

If the child has emotional problems which are affecting his school work or behaviour, he may be sent to a Child Guidance Clinic. Children can also be referred there by their General Practitioner. Sometimes the clinic will want to see the parents as well. The child may attend the clinic on a regular basis to undergo therapy to help him with his emotional problems and the school will usually receive a report on the child at the end of his treatment.

Social Services

If child abuse is suspected it is usually the Social Services who will be informed immediately by your Headteacher. The Social Services have the powers to investigate the family background of the child, interview the child and his parents, arrange for a medical examination of the child and remove the child to a 'place of safety' if it is thought that the child needs immediate protection.

Another area where the teacher may have to liaise with the Social Services is when you notice signs of poverty within a family and realise that the family are possibly not receiving all the benefits to which they are entitled. Although the teacher can contact Social Services about a family in need, often their staff are very overworked and the initiative is supposed to come from the claimant. It is here that (with an immense amount of tact) the teacher can help.

The School Medical Service

A School Nurse and School Doctor will visit the school regularly to give certain children medicals. These children may be chosen at random but they may also be examined because you feel that there is cause for concern. For example, you may be worried about the sight of a child or that a child is underweight or not growing properly.

School Nurses will also carry out head inspections but these have ceased to be a regular occurrence in many areas due to economic pressures.

If it is found that a child has a medical problem the parents are informed. If the parents are unconcerned and do not follow up the recommendation of the School Doctor, he may contact the child's General Practitioner or refer the child to a specialist himself.

The Police

Many Police forces operate a liaison scheme with schools where a representative (usually uniformed) from the Police force will visit the school on a regular basis to talk about the work of the police within the community and to advise children on subjects such as road safety and not talking to strangers.

Unhappily you may be involved with the police because your school has been broken into or because one of your children has broken the law. In cases such as this there will be close liaison between the Social Services, the Police and your Headteacher or his representative.

Voluntary Organisations

Many voluntary organisations are very pleased to be involved with the Education Service. Some organisations will assist you if you have a child in your class who has a problem in which they specialize. Examples of these are the Royal National Institute for the Deaf and societies dealing with medical problems such as diabetes and asthma.

You may have to liaise with some voluntary agencies if the family are experiencing problems and are receiving help from the agency. The NSPCC may be involved in a case of child abuse.

Another agency with which you may wish to liaise is the church of the family. If the family belong to a strict religious sect you will wish to respect their views and cause the least embarrassment to the child if it is necessary that at times he is treated differently from the other children.

What Happens Next

Statementing Children

If it is felt that a child has special educational needs, a 'statement' of these needs may be written by the Local Authority. This is a lengthy process involving reports on the child from various parties concerned such as the school's Psychological Service, the school and the parents.

The child's statement is reviewed annually and the special provision for the child such as support from the Special Educational Needs Support Team or the use of a Welfare Assistant may be adjusted accordingly.

Case Conferences

Once grounds for concern over a particular child have been established a Case Conference will be held. The conference members will consist of a representative from agencies who are currently, or will be in the future, involved with the child or his family. This will include your Headteacher. The parents of the child are not invited. The aim of the case conference is that all agencies share their knowledge of the child and his family and that a programme for the future can be set up to deal with the problems the child/family are experiencing. There may be further Case Conferences to review the situation at regular intervals.

As a result of a Case Conference the child's name may be entered on the Central Register of Child Abuse. You should be informed if any children in your class are on his register as you should be particularly sensitive to their vulnerability to abuse and be doubly vigilant. Any suspicions you have regarding a child who is registered should be reported immediately.

Welfare or Non-teaching Assistants

As a result of a recommendation in the child's statement or because the child is known to have other problems e.g. a physical handicap you may have the resource of a Welfare Assistant in your classroom. A Welfare Assistant is employed to free you from the extra time that such a child demands so that you can concentrate on his education and the education of the rest of the class. Therefore it is very difficult to define the role of the Welfare Assistant within the classroom because her job will vary according to the specific needs of the child for which she is employed. She may need specific first-aid or medical knowledge (such as how to use a nebuliser).

Many Welfare Assistants are women who have children of their own and wish to return to some form of employment which fits in with their children's school times. They may be mothers themselves and perhaps more confident than the inexperienced class teacher at dealing with 'accidents' and with helping children to dress and undress. Some Welfare Assistants enjoy teaching and many go on to teacher training.

Some teachers find the thought of a Welfare Assistant in the classroom a potentially threatening situation. The job of the teacher is especially vulnerable to criticism. It is important that the Welfare Assistant has an awareness of her professional responsibility towards the class teacher and the school. She must also accept that her role in the classroom will always be secondary to that of the class teacher. Much of the relationship between teacher and Welfare Assistant will depend on the personalities involved but a few guidelines may help.

1 Make sure that the role of your Welfare Assistant is clearly defined so that both of you, and the children, know in which areas she can be used as a resource and in which areas they are to come to you.

2 Expect support from your Welfare Assistant and in turn give her yours. If you have to contradict something she has done or said explain to the child that Mrs Z wasn't wrong, there are two ways of doing this and you would like him to do it this way. The children may try to play you off one against the other — this will be much harder for them to do if you and your Welfare Assistant support each other or if there is a clear role differentiation between you.

3 Brief your Welfare Assistant as to your plans for the term/week/day so that she knows what is happening and can support you. For example, if you inform her that you intend to take the children pond dipping on the first nice afternoon it gives her the opportunity to make sure that she has trousers and wellington boots in school.

4 If possible give her her own base in the classroom where she can sit and work. This may be in close proximity to the child she has to help.

5 It is often difficult to draw the line between the role of the Welfare Assistant and the teacher, especially when dealing with a child with learning difficulties. But it would usually be the teacher who would plan and initiate a programme of work and the Welfare Assistant who would provide the adult support that the child would need to carry the work through e.g. showing flashcards, playing games, finding the right book/crayons/materials for the next piece of work. In this circumstance it is important that adequate records are kept so that all adults concerned with the child — class teacher, Welfare Assistant and Special Needs Teacher — are all aware of the child's programme of work, what he has achieved to date and the problems encountered. On the following page is a form of record-keeping which has been popular in my present school.

Nursery Nurses

Some Nursery and Infant Classes are fortunate enough to have the services of a Nursery Nurse. Her role is similar to that of a Welfare Assistant because she is also there to assist you in the time-consuming tasks involved in caring for young children so that you can concentrate on your teaching. There is, however, a major difference between a Welfare Assistant and a Nursery Nurse. The latter is a professional person who has undergone training in the care of young children. Although many of the guidelines I have given for dealing with a Welfare Assistant will also apply to a Nursery Nurse, the teacher must remember she is dealing with a trained professional who will not be terribly happy washing paint-pots all week!

Week Ending 15. 5. 89.	COMMENTS
FUZZ BUZZ 3 — THE GARDEN. Read p. 9-13. Use sentence maker. Flash cards for difficult words.	Absent Monday 11.5.89. Difficulty with 'these', 'comes', & 'under.' Up to page 12.
MATHS — Ginn 2 Bk 2 Continue working through book Money value sheets 3. 1. 2.	12. 5. 89. — needs practice with tens & units — days of week correct.
DAILY DIARY Two sentences and a picture to include full stops and capital letters.	13. 5. 89. — sheet 3.2. finished — sheet 3.3. up to 20p.
SOUNDS. Th, br. cr. DEVISE Days of week.	14. 5. 89. Comes, down, under for homework. 15. 5. 89. — sheet. 3.3. finished — read to page 13

THE 'TRAFFIC LIGHT SYSTEM' for individual words/sounds.

WORD	1/2/89	16/2/89	20/2/89
Pat	G	G	G
they	G	R	R
are	R	Y	Y
water	G	G	G
come	Y	G	G

G — green dot — word known.

R — red dot — word unknown.

Y — yellow dot — word attempted or half known.

33

Day to Day Routine

Keeping them occupied

No matter which teaching method you prefer you will have to know exactly what each child should have achieved by the end of the day (or week in some cases). This requires organisation. Children are keen to learn but they are not angels. If you give them the opportunity to mess about because they have nothing to do, everyone, except the goody-goodies, will take it. Therefore you will need something to occupy their time once they have finished their set tasks. Try a 'Personal Topic', (own choice, within reason), a set of workcards, (not terribly popular but educationally valid, especially if you make your own), a 'continuous story' (Aren't they all? I hear you mutter, only this one is in a book of its own and goes on and on and on . . . . .), or some maths or language/reading games (LDA and Macmillan have some super games, or make your own with ideas from NARE). It is not a good idea to give the child more tasks, he'll only work slower in future! However do be prepared for widely different results. The child who works incredibly slowly will only have written his name on the front of his continuous story book. Hide it on parent's evening and don't worry — these tasks are meant to be supplementary to the main core of your teaching.

Getting them in

The main methods of introducing the children into the classroom are these.

1 Let the children come in at will, sit down and do a task or read quietly until you arrive.

All right in theory but difficult in practice, especially with certain classes. If you (or the school) insist upon this make sure they know exactly what they have to do when they come in and lock away all scissors and precious items. If your classroom is inside the school building make sure you have steel tips on your shoes so that they can hear you coming and stop any nonsense before you arrive — much better than catching them at it and giving up a well-earned break keeping them in. But this method does have the advantage that your class is all ready for you when you arrive and you can even insist they stand up when you enter the room.

2 The children line up outside the door until you arrive and then file in.

This is difficult if your classroom is outside. They'll get very cold and wet if you're not on time and you'll get cold and wet seeing them in. If they are noisy the whole school will know but at least you can keep them out in the cold and wet until they are quiet! You may find it easier to tell them their work before you let them in so they get out the requisite book before they sit down.

Registration

Always have something for them to do when they enter the classroom. During registration my class have a 'Quick Test' of ten questions on the chalkboard which they do in silence while I sort out the registers and deal with problems. The Quick Test has two great advantages. Firstly it keeps them quiet, and secondly it can be used to reinforce work that they did a short while ago or to improve their general knowledge. Here are a few examples from a Quick Test Book.

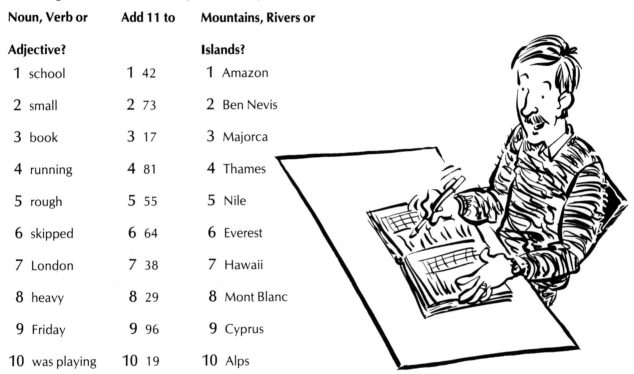

Noun, Verb or Adjective?	Add 11 to	Mountains, Rivers or Islands?
1 school	1 42	1 Amazon
2 small	2 73	2 Ben Nevis
3 book	3 17	3 Majorca
4 running	4 81	4 Thames
5 rough	5 55	5 Nile
6 skipped	6 64	6 Everest
7 London	7 38	7 Hawaii
8 heavy	8 29	8 Mont Blanc
9 Friday	9 96	9 Cyprus
10 was playing	10 19	10 Alps

▷ (**A quick tip:** It's very difficult to think of random numbers for a test like this. Instead write the numbers 0–9 randomly in the units column. Do the same in the tens and hundreds columns and you will have a random list of numbers covering all digits).

There are several methods of taking the register. Here are a few which work, with their pros and cons.

1 Teacher calls out name of child. Child responds with 'Good Morning Miss So and So', 'Yes' or 'Present'.

The advantage of this is that it is fairly quick and it teaches them 'Good Morning/Afternoon' as a polite greeting. However it is easy to make a mistake if you

have a dozy child in the class who doesn't respond as you are whizzing your red marks down the register. If you wish, you can adapt this idea to reinforce sounds or rhythms found in the children's names. They have to copy the sound/rhythm in their reply. You can also do this by singing to help improve their pitch and memory.

2   The children call out their name or a number in order. Where there is a break in the sequence a child is absent.

This is very quick, can be used to reinforce counting and to teach ordinal numbers 'First, Second, Third . . . etc.' However, it can be a little impersonal.

The worst thing about a Monday morning is probably the dinner register. If you are lucky the school secretary may come round and collect the dinner money. If you are unlucky you will have to deal with this yourself. The traditional way of dealing with collecting money from children is to call the children out one by one. This can be very time consuming and children who have no money to pay become bored and restless (and we all know what that means). An alternative method is to take the dinner register where each child responds 'Dinners/Sandwiches/Homes, please' (note it's never 'home'!) but children with money say 'Dinner Money, please.' At the end of the register the children with money line up in the same order that they are in the register and you take their money in while the rest of the class get on with their work. In the front of my register I write how much dinner money should be collected for 1–10 days as I'm not very good at working out 8 days at 68p in my head.

Assemblies

Most schools have their assembly in the morning after registration which means that you have to be organised with your register or you will always be last! The task of taking the assembly usually falls to the Headteacher or another senior member of staff and before you moan about hearing the story of little Suzy for the third time this year think how much you would like to take assembly for the whole school most days. Most teachers would admit that taking assembly is one of the worst tasks they can be asked to do and we all know why. It is one of the very few occasions when we are asked to perform in front of our colleagues. Most of us are quite happy to take assembly with only the children. When the class teacher has to take assembly, it usually involves the children and is a class assembly. However it is difficult for these not to develop into some form of competition and one must beware of spending a disproportionate amount of time on their preparation and rehearsal. One of the easiest ways of avoiding this is to have an assembly based on work the class is currently involved in. Make your assembly entertaining with a bit of audience participation and you can't fail!

Moving children from place to place

In the course of the school day you may need to leave your classroom and take your children to another part of the building. The following tips may help you achieve this with the minimum of disturbance to others.

1   Tell the children where they are going and why. If it is something nice i.e. TV or PE threaten them with a cancellation of the lesson if they misbehave on the way or, conversely, tell them they will be rewarded with a PE lesson or TV programme if they are good and do not disturb any other classes.

2 Tell the children to line up at the door, quietly in pairs. Infants and younger children may need to hold hands with their partner.

3 Wait, or yell, for the hubbub to subside. Make sure that the front pair are trustworthy. No-one leaves the room until there is silence. Remind children of the consequences of misbehaviour or reward for good behaviour.

4 If necessary, choose someone to hold open the door. Tell the front pair to lead off. Watch the first part of the class move off.

5 Leave the room about half-way down the class line so that you can keep an eye on the back and the front.

6 If the children have to travel round a corner, stand at that corner so that you can still see all your class at the same time. If there is another corner soon afterwards, make a rule that the children pause there until the end of the class have passed the first corner and you say they may proceed.

7 Make sure the children know exactly what they have to do upon entering the new room i.e. where to sit/get changed etc.

After a while this will become second nature to both you and your class but do punish any offenders hard. A few PE lessons spent practising moving around as a class will soon bring most children to their senses.

Dismissing the Class

Your class is working hard and it is time to pack up. This is one of the times when they can take advantage of you if you give them the opportunity. You have to make it absolutely clear what they have to do and, if possible, have as few children out of their places at any one time as you can.

Here are some ways to do this.

1 Call for silence. Explain packing-up procedure. No-one moves until you say so.

2 Monitors collect in books and/or other equipment. Children tidy up their desks/tables.

3 Children put their own property away a group at a time.

4 Don't get sidetracked yourself. Stand and watch them. Then you will have witnessed who shoved whom.

5 Make encouraging noises like 'I wonder who will be the first table ready?' or 'The first table ready can go out to play first'. (Why do they fall for this every time?)

6 Insist that all is quiet before you dismiss them.

7 If you have a clock in the classroom now is a good time to discuss the time (sorry). Ask them what the time will be when they return to the classroom, or where the hands will be at the end of the lunch-time. This also works when you are giving them their work. 'We are going to stop in half an hour and have a story. Where will the big hand be in half an hour?'

To avoid pandemonium there are various strategies to dismissing the class at the end of the lesson.

Individually

This is useful for when you are all standing there looking at each other and you realise that there is another five minutes until the bell. Try giving the children a 'QQ' (Quick Quiz to the uninitiated). First person to put their hand up answers the question. If they get it right they stand by the door and can go home first. For some reason children adore this and I suppose it is good for extending their general knowledge or revising work done. However, it does give you brain ache at the end of a hard day to think of thirty-odd general knowledge questions that an eight-year-old can answer.

By Groups

Probably the most common way. When everyone is ready dismiss a group at a time. This needn't be where they are sitting. You can have 'All children with black shoes' etc.

Awkward Lessons

If we are honest, some lessons are a lot easier than others. This is because some lessons give the children greater opportunity to test your discipline than others so I am going to deal with those lessons under the heading of 'awkward'.

Art and Craft

The thought of the children running riot with scissors, glue, craft-knives and drawing ink (indelible, of course) is enough to send most teachers reaching for the valium. Indeed, many prefer to stick to the simple things in life and the children do much of their art work with a pencil or felt-tips. So here are a few ideas for the more courageous among us.

1 Don't have all the children doing art/craft at the same time if you can help it. This keeps the problem down to manageable proportions.

2 Get help if you can. Many parents would prefer to be involved helping with craft/cookery than listening to readers.

3 Have monitors to put out everything before the lesson begins. It is easier if you limit the amount of paint the children are given. Some teachers just give red, blue and yellow so the children have to mix all their colours. This is both practical and educational, but not really suitable for very young children.

4 Nobody touches anything until told. ('Sit on hands' could be employed/ threatened here.)

5 The children who finish early can do their own washing up, but when the majority have finished you will need monitors. Ask for volunteers or offer the job as a reward. I had a near riot on my hands in my first art lesson when I told two naughty children that they could do the washing-up as a punishment!

6 The children take their washing-up to the sink (or buckets if you have no sink) in groups. Make each group responsible for clearing up their table but you will probably need someone to oversee the putting away of the newspaper.

7 It helps if you can have a place in the room where the wet paintings can dry, or sabotage may occur.

8 The quality of the children's work will be greatly improved if you are able to demonstrate/have an example of what you want them to do. To this end keep a few pieces of the best work to show the next time you do that lesson. Unfortunately, for the first lesson you will have to do it yourself!

9 Try to provide your class with a variety of brush sizes. Try using their brushes yourself — if you, as an adult, are unable to control the brush to a satisfactory standard, then it will be impossible for a child — time to ask for new paintbrushes.

PE

1 After the children have finished changing, make sure they know exactly what they have to do e.g. sit down quietly, practise a known activity, get out some apparatus etc.

2 When planning lessons it is easier to begin with individual activities moving to working in pairs and then larger groups rather than mixing them up.

3 When giving the children instructions don't tell them that they will need a partner/group of four, or they will spend your precious explanation time grabbing their friends to make the requisite-sized group. Tell them at the beginning and wait until they have sorted themselves out, or tell them at the end.

4 Choosing teams:
   a) You choose the captains and let them take turns in choosing their teams. This may give you uneven teams. It is not very nice for the children who are always chosen last.
   b) You choose the teams, trying to keep things even by telling each child 'bat' or 'field'. If more than two teams are required choose one child to be a captain of each team and number the teams. These children then stand in order in a line holding up the number of fingers corresponding to their team number (for obvious reasons you can insist they use two hands). The rest of the class are then each given a number and they have to stand behind the child holding up the number you have given them.

These methods are quick and usually more balanced.

5 Getting out apparatus
   a) **Games:** Either have monitors responsible for getting out and putting away a particular piece of apparatus or make each child responsible for something. Bands are collected in more easily if they are looped over an outstretched arm, not given hand to hand.
   b) **Gymnastics:** To avoid a general free for all, an alternative is to group the children (I usually name them after famous gymnasts or countries). Give each group a small card with a diagram of the apparatus that you wish them get out. On the back list the apparatus needed as shown.

The card is given back to you when the children have finished getting out the apparatus.
   This has the advantage that every child knows exactly what he has to get out and

where it is to be placed. It is also easy for you to change the apparatus arrangements from lesson to lesson, without lengthy explanation.

Once the apparatus has been set out the children sit on the floor quietly and wait for you to come and check it. Once you have decreed it safe then you can give them their activities and the lesson can start. Having the apparatus in groups also means that the children work on one group of apparatus at a time and only move on at your direction. This stops queues for the more popular apparatus and overloaded wallbars.

6 Putting away apparatus

When putting the apparatus away, the mats usually go away first. It is easier if the children queue up to put the mats away rather than approaching from all directions. The rest of the apparatus can then be safely put away. When a group has finished putting away its apparatus, the children sit down quietly out of the way until told to go and change. This way you will not be left with three keen children and half a hall-full of apparatus to put away.

7 When watching a gymnastics lesson, you can observe more of the room if you stand in a corner.

8 At the end of the lesson try not to dismiss the whole class/group at the same time. Dismiss them by group, or set an activity to do first which will stagger their dismissal.

Music

1 If you wish all the children to have an instrument, let them choose their instruments a group at a time. A different group to go first each lesson.

2 No-one touches their instrument unless told to play it. Putting them on the floor until needed helps with self-discipline.

3 Triangles always seem to be minus their beaters. A pair of scissors is a good substitute.

4 Do not assume that the children know how to play untuned percussion instruments. A quick demonstration can improve the quality of the sound.

Giving the children their work

You will already have some idea of the work the children should be doing from your lesson plans — but how do you tell them? After introducing your lesson, go over the work that you expect the children to do. The more detailed the better. Go over examples if you can. Be precise as to how long they have to fulfil their task (see lesson planning). If possible, have a record of the work somewhere to which the child can refer. This may be in a book or on the chalkboard. It sometimes helps to leave your examples on the chalkboard and any spellings which you think that they may need.

Giving out and collecting books

It is occasions such as these when control of a difficult class can be lost so you must know what you are doing.

▷ **Collecting books:** Books can be collected in by a monitor — any handy, trusted child — or given in individually. Make sure everyone knows who is collecting the books and that they remain in their places while the books are being collected. It causes immediate chaos if children enthusiastically get out of their places and give their book to your chosen collector-in. It helps if the books are given in open at the page which is to be marked and the same way up. Giving in books individually can be part of the general tidying up process or they can give them in on their way out of the classroom or when they have finished that piece of work. Another method is to have a child collect the books from each group/row of children.

Many teachers have found that 'Put your books on my desk,' is not a good idea. Most teachers' desks resemble the church jumble sale on a good day, with notes from parents, bits of lost property, confiscated toys and bits of lego picked up from the floor. It's very easy to lose Mary's maths book among the debris which causes frayed nerves, bad temper, acute embarrassment and an overall waste of time next Maths lesson. An idea is to have a box/tray/small basket for unmarked books and another one for marked books. Even if you have already marked some of the books during the lesson time, insist upon all books being given in. A quick count will tell you whether someone has not bothered to give their book in. This saves you time going through your record book checking off names.

▷ **Giving out books:** The quickest person at giving out books is the teacher but while you are thus occupied trouble can brew so a regular monitor or trusted child is the next best thing. It is better to have more than one child giving out books at a time. If you have a tray for marked books, the monitor can come in early in the morning and give them out before school starts. This causes the least disruption of all. It is quicker if the books have been given in in groups because then they can be given back in groups. If the children are regularly going to be giving out their own books it is advisable for you to write their names on the fronts of their books. Children find it very difficult to read the immature handwriting of another child.

Marking

On a simple level, books are marked so that you and the child know whether he has the work right or wrong. If he has the work correct then you know he has understood it and is ready for the next stage. If he has the work wrong then you know he has not understood it and needs more re-inforcement. Unfortunately life is not all that simple. One would hope that a child would learn from constructive marking and not be disillusioned. Yet we still hand back to them pages covered in red ink. Some teachers prefer to mark in pencil or black ink as it seems less traumatic. The best way to mark work is with the child beside you. Then you can explain things to him as you correct his work and also find out his reasoning behind a mistake which is not clear. However, there is not usually enough time for this so most of us write what we hope are constructive comments at the bottom of the piece of work. But this does require a certain level of reading ability and maturity on the part of the child. There are some excellent stickers available to praise and encourage children. Most primary teachers do not give a grade but they do reward effort, perhaps with a sticker, star, house-point or small sweet. (It doesn't take long for my new class to work out that ICB stands for one chocolate button).

When marking a piece of work which is incorrect try to find out what it is that the child has misunderstood so that you can help him next lesson. When marking a piece of written work don't mark every mistake. Choose one or two particular errors and correct all of those. Some teachers list common spelling errors at the bottom of a piece of written work for the child to write out a certain number of times (usually three to five). Handwriting errors can be dealt with in the same way.

In certain circumstances the children can mark their own work and then hand it in to you for checking. This is not laziness on the part of the teacher. The children can learn a lot from marking their own work and discovering their own mistakes. Most children will not cheat and you will soon spot those that do and increase your omnipotence in the eyes of your class.

Most primary teachers would prefer to reward good work than to punish poor, but sometimes a child has deliberately wasted his time and needs to be punished. The simplest thing is to make him re-do the piece of work, preferably in his own time (i.e. playtime or lunch time — although this isn't always a punishment in the winter months). If this fails, sending him home with the work and a note to his parents asking that the work be done sometimes has the desired result. If the child's work is constantly poor, there may be an underlying reason and no punishment is going to change this. For how to deal with this situation please see the section on Discipline.

Fire Practices

These are an infrequent but very necessary part of school life. You must be sure of exactly what to do because in the event of a real emergency the children will look to you for guidance.

When the fire bell goes off

1 Don't be seen to panic. And don't let the children know you're annoyed because the fire practice has spoilt your best lesson this term.

2 Tell certain children to close the windows. If you have a class pet you should make someone responsible for taking it outside as well.

3 Tell the class to line up. I ask my class to line up in register order: it takes no longer for them to do and it is much quicker for me to take the register outside.

4 Pick up your handbag/wallet and the register.

5 Tell the children to lead off to the assembly point.

6 When the children are lined up go down the line taking the register. This way you can see if the child is present and you do not have to rely on a small voice from the back of the line.

7 Report your class numbers to whoever is responsible for this.

Being On Supply

There are great advantages and disadvantages to being a supply teacher. You do not have the extra responsibilities of the full-time classroom teacher, but you are in a more insecure position because you do not know the children. A wonderful arrangement is if you can supply for a school at which you used to teach.

If you wish to supply teach you can either contact your local Area Education Office who probably have a list of supply teachers (which should be updated regularly) or you can contact individual schools in your area or you can do both. If you are new to the supply situation you will find that schools will contact you when

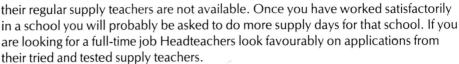

their regular supply teachers are not available. Once you have worked satisfactorily in a school you will probably be asked to do more supply days for that school. If you are looking for a full-time job Headteachers look favourably on applications from their tried and tested supply teachers.

Often Headteachers will ask each other for the names of good supply teachers. If you are available at short notice i.e. 8.55 am and you can travel, you will probably have many requests for supply work. This does mean, however, that you have to be ready to go at a moment's notice so no lie-ins — and have your bag packed in readiness.

Having done my fair share of supply work and starting work in new schools I have developed a list of items which are absolutely necessary to know/have available before the children arrive. If you are ever in the same situation you may find the following useful:

Things to know

Where to find both adult and children's lavatories.
Where the stock cupboard is and the arrangements for finding certain things such as:

▷ art paper

▷ Maths or English exercise books (somebody always finished one the day that I was on supply)

▷ plain and lined paper (the drawer was always empty when I was on supply)

▷ The school times (don't ever ask the children)

▷ The name (surname as well — children are very obtuse when it comes to 'The second year teacher with blonde hair' introduced to you as Mary) of one member of staff on whom to call for assistance or information if needed

▷ Arrangements for playground duty

▷ How they change their reading books

▷ Arrangements for dismissal at the end of the day

▷ If there are any children with special medical needs

I always take with me the equipment necessary for the day's lessons.

▷ scissors

▷ spare rulers

▷ spare pencils

▷ story book

▷ quizbook

▷ sellotape

▷ red and black biros (for the register)

▷ whistle

▷ plimsolls (in case they've forgotten to tell you its Miss X's turn to take the whole of the fourth year for PE on Wednesday afternoons — or because the weather is fine).

Medical Problems

Before meeting your new class try to be aware of any children with specific medical problems and how this may affect their life in school. If necessary, you should also know what to do with the child in case of an emergency. The following is a list of some of the more common medical conditions affecting children and their effect on the child's school life.

Hearing Difficulties

The child will have to sit near the front of the class, preferably directly in front of you so that he can use your lips as a clue to what you are saying. If the child has grommets (a small plastic tube fitted into the eardrum to allow the middle ear to drain) fitted then he may not be allowed to go swimming.

If you suspect that a child in your class has hearing difficulties try the following tests. Without the child being aware of your presence, stand behind him and say his name quietly. He should be able to hear the familiar sound of his name above the background noise of the class. If he does not turn round, repeat his name becoming louder until he does hear you.

Another method is to stand the child in front of you with his back towards you. Explain to the child that you are going to say some words and you want him to tell you whether you are saying two different words, or the same word twice. Read the following list of words, one pair at a time, noting his answers. Try to read the list in a low voice so you do not give clues by emphasising certain words.

pet-bet	bad-dab
peach-teach	got-got
wash-wash	mate-meat
nice-mice	name-mane
sink-think	other-over
of-of	will-win
tall-tell	sun-sun
net-ten	cub-cup

If you feel that there may be a hearing problem, ask for the child to be seen by the school doctor or nurse on their next visit, or speak to the parents.

Sight Problems

The most common of these (long-sightedness, short-sightedness and squints) will be corrected by wearing glasses. Most children usually hate wearing their glasses and you may need to remind them and insist that they be worn. Children wearing glasses for the first time need to be treated with great sensitivity. Don't bring their glasses to the general attention of the class, but a quiet word from you on how nice they look can work wonders for their self-confidence.

A child who has sight problems may show certain characteristics.

1 He may hold his book at arm's length.

2 He may hold his book very close to his face.

3 He may screw up his eyes to look at the chalkboard.

4 He may complain of headaches.

5 He may have a very short concentration span when faced with written work.

6 He may have problems with word recognition in reading.

However, many children with poor eyesight do not realise that the rest of us can see clearly and do not complain.

If you suspect that a child in your class may have difficulties in seeing clearly, ask the school doctor or nurse to check him the next time they visit, or have a word with his parents.

Asthma

If the child's asthma is caused by an allergy you will need to ensure that the child does not come into contact with the class hamster, his friend's sweets or whatever it is which may trigger an attack. Most parents are very informative over the danger signs leading up to an attack so you will know what to look out for. Try to keep asthmatic children away from radiators when the heating is on and, if the weather is very cold, don't send him outside to play. Try to find an excuse to keep him in the classroom.

The medical treatment the child receives will depend on the severity and frequency of the attacks. The child may have a small hand-held inhalent which will spray a drug to relieve a minor attack, or he may need a small, briefcase-sized nebuliser for more severe attacks. He will probably be well used to using either of these, but in the case of small children you may feel happier knowing how to use them as well.

Asthmatic children are encouraged to participate in all areas of physical activity, but need understanding when they may ask to sit out half-way through a lesson. Strongly determined children may need watching that they do not seriously over-exert themselves. Children are more likely to have asthma attacks on cold, dry days than warm, moist days.

Allergies

Allergies can cause a variety of symptoms in children from asthma attacks to the cold-like symptoms of hay-fever. In certain children an allergy may alter their behaviour in that they become irritable, tearful, very active and have a short concentration span. If this happens to a child in your class try to channel the excess energy into physical activity i.e. taking a message round the school, tidying up a cupboard, clearing up the sink area. Make sure that the child knows the bounds of acceptable behaviour concerning other children and their property but help him by not putting him into situations where trouble could occur.

Sometimes the child may behave oddly, such as hiding under a table. Try not to make a fuss or come into direct conflict with the child. Try to encourage him out with the promise of some pleasurable activity and if that fails leave him where he is with a book to read, some colouring to do, or to sleep until the attack has passed.

Epilepsy

This can be divided into two main forms.

▷ **Grand Mal:** In this form of epilepsy the child may suddenly fall to the ground and be unconscious for several minutes. His limbs and the muscles of the face may jerk. After an attack the child may pass into normal sleep.

▷ **Petit Mal:** With this form the child does not lose consciousness but may appear to be day-dreaming. The eyes may glaze over and the child will not respond to things going on around him. The attacks usually last from 10 to 15 seconds and the child will not have any recollection of what has happened when he returns to normal consciousness.

If you have a child with grand mal in your class it can be disturbing for the other children to see an attack. They will follow your lead so you must keep calm, remove anything which may cause the child injury and lay the child on his front with his head turned to one side in the 'recovery position'. Do not put anything into the child's mouth and do not try to restrain him. Reassure the rest of the class and send for help, if needed.

Diabetes

The child will be on a strict diet and this should be remembered when giving out rewards and end of term treats. Most diabetic children can be given alternative sweets made for diabetics and available from chemists. A diabetic child will also have to eat frequently and may need to munch something during lesson time. This needs to be dealt with sensitively for if the child feels embarrassed or different he may not eat when he needs to, with very serious consequences. It is only politeness if the child asks first if he may eat something and a light-hearted remark from you will go a long way to easing his embarrassment.

There are many more medical disorders which you may meet in the course of your career but these are the most common. Usually the rest of the class are very eager to help if the problems are explained to them clearly. If not they may wonder why John is allowed to eat biscuits in Maths lessons and the rest of them are not. If they realise a child has a medical difficulty that he is overcoming they are usually proud to help the child and very, very rarely do they poke fun at him.

Bereavement

I hope that you will never have to suffer the death of a member of your class or your school, but if you do I hope the following may be of some help and comfort.

Try to make sure that the child's close friends know before they hear the news at school. They will be upset and it is kinder if they are at home with their parents to support them.

Do tell the class as much as you feel they ought to know (perhaps what the child died of, where he died, time and place of the funeral etc.). Be natural with the children, grief is an important part of the healing process. Give them time to grieve as well. On a practical basis have tissues handy for very upset children.

Most children (especially if they are very young) will not understand the implications of death. They may well be upset simply because of the atmosphere in the school. Older children may need help in coming to terms with the realities of death. An excellent book to read to them, or let them borrow, is 'Grandpa and Me' (Marlee and Benny Alex, Lion Publishing) which deals with this situation with great sensitivity.

Try to keep the day as normal as possible. Children who are upset will need the security of the normal school routine. If there is a brother or sister in the school the children must be encouraged to help them in their sorrow. Many children (and adults) feel embarrassed dealing with someone in a time of trial. Help the children to understand that, although unhappy, the brother or sister will need their friendship now, more than ever.

It was obviously unsuitable for the children to attend the funeral of the little boy who died in my class, much as they wanted to. However, at the request of his parents, we taped them singing some of the child's favourite hymns, which was played during the funeral. In this way the children did not feel left out and it formed a very moving part of the service.

Illness

Frequently children will become ill at school. Most LEAs lay down strict rules as to what medical treatment can be given to children while at school (usually none). There is usually someone responsible for dealing with sick children in the school (usually one of the administrative staff) so if a child complains of nausea, headache or general malaise it is usually wise to send them to this person, accompanied by another child if possible.

Under the new regulations you should not come into contact with any bodily fluids and there should be an 'AIDS Pack' somewhere with plastic aprons, plastic gloves and plastic bags for disposing of all rubbish when you have finished dealing with the child. This is all very well in theory but it is hard to restrain your natural enthusiasm to get things cleared up as soon as possible when someone has made a puddle on your floor or has a nose-bleed running down their face. It seems callous to say 'Hang on while I get the pack', but this is what you must do. If children become used to first aid treatment this way now, then it won't seem quite so obvious when it becomes really necessary. You should also make sure that any visible open wounds that you have yourself are covered as well, just in case.

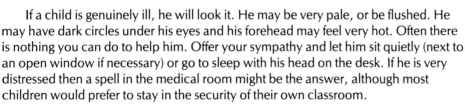

If a child is genuinely ill, he will look it. He may be very pale, or be flushed. He may have dark circles under his eyes and his forehead may feel very hot. Often there is nothing you can do to help him. Offer your sympathy and let him sit quietly (next to an open window if necessary) or go to sleep with his head on the desk. If he is very distressed then a spell in the medical room might be the answer, although most children would prefer to stay in the security of their own classroom.

Many children will have vague headaches and tummy upsets if they are worried about something. The symptoms may or may not be genuine but in this case it is better to treat the cause and not the symptom! If the cause is obvious, such as a test, tell the child they can go to the medical room after they have done the test but you want them to do that first. You understand that they are not feeling well and you will make allowances for this. Usually there will be a miraculous recovery.

If you are sure that a child is not genuinely ill but there is no obvious reason why, tell him to sit alone, quietly for a while. An ill child will be grateful for the peace, a well child will become bored very quickly. Playtimes can be used to your advantage. Either, 'Well, if you are too ill to do PE I don't think you're well enough to run around the playground, do you?' or 'As you are not feeling very well I think that some fresh air will do you good — make sure that you wrap up warm.' In either case the child's snack for play-time would not be a 'good idea'. Again, recovery is usually instant.

Common Childhood Infectious Diseases

▷ **Chicken pox:** The child has a fever with red, raised itchy spots which turn into blisters and then scabs. These are mainly found on the face, neck, chest and back.
Incubation Period 14–21 days
Infectious from 5 days before the spots appear until they have become scabs.

▷ **Measles:** Fever, cough, runny nose, red, blotchy rash on face and body.
Incubation Period 7–14 days
Infectious from appearance of first symptoms to four days after the rash appears.

▷ **Mumps:** Swelling of glands on one or both sides of the upper neck, fever, sore throat.
Incubation Period 12–21 days
Infectious from three days after the glands swell to about seven days after the swelling has gone.

▷ **German Measles (Rubella):** Low temperature, swollen glands in the neck, mottled red rash on face, neck and chest.
Incubation Period 14–21 days
Infectious from 7 days before appearance of the rash until four days after.

No child should be in school if it is known to have an infectious disease but if you think that a child has German Measles then all expectant mums (parents and staff) should be told.

A child should not be in school (and neither should a teacher) with any of the following.

▷ Headlice

▷ Impetigo

▷ Scabies

▷ Ringworm on the head and scalp (Ringworm on the body is different and only needs to be kept covered)

▷ Conjunctivitis

▷ Pulmonary Thrombosis

▷ Dysentery

▷ Diphtheria

▷ Food Poisoning

▷ Infective Jaundice

▷ Meningitis

▷ Poliomyelitis

▷ Typhoid Fever

▷ Whooping Cough

▷ Threadworms

This is a very general list. If you are in any doubt please consult your doctor.

Your school office should have a detailed list of the communicable diseases which your county consider warrant exclusion from school.

Calls of Nature

Most infants should be toilet trained by the time they arrive at school. But in case you come across one that isn't and you are not used to dealing with this aspect of young children, here are some helpful hints.

Most children have a fear of falling down the toilet, especially if their feet are unable to reach the floor. Therefore girls tend to perch on the edge of the seat which means that they may wet the seat, their legs and underwear. To avoid this by making sure that the child sits back far enough, encourage the child to hold onto the seat on either side. Boys whilst sitting on the toilet will need to make sure that everything is pointing downwards as usually they will pass water as well and if this isn't done then they will spray everything in sight! It is sometimes easier for children to wipe themselves clean after they have got down from the toilet.

Boys will urinate facing the toilet. The child has to take hold of himself firmly either using the first two fingers scissor action or using both hands. The hold must be firm or the child will not have any directional control. When the child has finished passing water he must give one or two shakes to get rid of excess water and replace everything comfortably inside pants and trousers, especially if trousers have a zip.

If you do have to help a child in this way, make sure that there is another child or adult as a witness to your activities. If you really don't feel confident enough to tackle this yourself, an alternative is to make sure that the child uses the toilet at the same time as others so that their methods (hopefully) are acquired by him.

Infants must be allowed to go to the toilet whenever they wish but by the time children reach the lower juniors they should be able to wait until the next playtime. Instinct will tell you whether a child really needs to go to the toilet or whether he is just bored. An obvious look of desperation and hopping about is not to be trifled with, but a calm request ten minutes after playtime has ended can be treated differently. One method of finding out if a child is genuine is to refuse the request. If the child asks again about ten minutes later then he really needs to go. Usually they go back to their place and trouble you no more. One word of warning; in cold weather children need to go to the toilet much more frequently, especially boys.

It is not a good idea to let more than one child go to the toilet at the same time — unless one of the children is ill. You will find that if you let one child go to the toilet, suddenly all the rest of the class wish to go. There is no answer to this except heartlessness.

Discipline, Punishments and Rewards

Discipline is something that concerns every teacher for if the class is not under control, teaching is very difficult. Good discipline will be developed by confidence and experience for it is the art of stopping them doing something you don't want them to do before they've done it (or even thought about it!).

In this chapter you will find a few ideas and pointers which may help if you are faced with discipline problems. You may feel that the ideas are unsympathetic. Many new teachers enter the profession with a love of children and wish to have their affection in return. They feel that if they are nice to the children then the children will be nice to them. Unfortunately, this is often not so. Some children will interpret this as a sign of weakness in their teacher and make their teacher's life a nightmare. Try to aim for the children's respect first. Once you have their respect then they will learn how much you care about them and then will care about you in return. Discipline alone will not earn you their respect, only their fear. Respect will come from a caring, just discipline tempered with an understanding of the child's world.

Getting off to a Good Start

The standard of your discipline is set from the moment your new class crosses the threshold. Be not lulled into a false sense of security by their grovelling 'Good mornings' and instant obedience to your every whim. It won't last unless you do something about it first. If you feel they might be a difficult class, or you are feeling

particularly insecure, before they have even entered your classroom find something to tell them off about. Anything will do — not lining up correctly/quietly/on time etc, etc. . . . When they are suitably chastened and the sensitive ones are wishing they were back with Mrs X, let them come in. Try to be extra firm for the first week or so and then you can begin to relax a bit and let them see you as your usual lovable self. By this time they will have a healthy respect for you so they are yours for the rest of the year. It is much easier to set very high standards to start with and then relax a little than to try to regain your standards later on.

Keeping the Good Start Going

The basis of good discipline is confidence. Remember you are in charge and what you say goes or else something unpleasant happens. (However, that does not licence you to go power mad.) Whatever you do with the children do it with confidence — even if it is wrong. If you make a mistake, congratulate the little creep who told you for spotting today's deliberate error, explain that you are not perfect and carry on. Do not get flustered if something goes wrong. If water goes everywhere in the art lesson get the children to clear it up. Make sure you are in the capacity of an overseer — if you get involved it gives them an opportunity to play up behind your back.

Make sure that the way you stand and act reflects your confidence (even if you don't have any). Try not to wear anything that you can fiddle with, scarf, beads etc., as that can give away your nervousness and be distracting for the children.

Children need to have parameters to their behaviour and will respect you if you lay down fair rules and stick to them. Children will misbehave if they feel something is unjust or they feel that there will be no consequences to their breaking of the rules. The secret is to be consistent. Early on in the year explain to your new class the rules of your classroom and the reason why those particular rules exist.

All early misdemeanours should be punished. Do not let anyone off because it was a first offence. If you punish now you will not have to punish again but you must be fair, or be seen to be fair in the eyes of the children. Remember what might appear to be a heinous crime to you may not appear so to them.

Never threaten a punishment you cannot carry out. If you threaten a punishment and your bluff is called you must do as you have threatened. Do not substitute or (even worse) let off with a warning. All their respect for you will be lost.

There will be times when you feel that you would like to warn the children first, especially in potentially troublesome situations. Tell them the consequences of misbehaviour and if they call your bluff, carry out your threat. If this seems unfair in the eyes of the children, for example they have all lost their playtime because two children were talking, keep all the class in for five minutes and then explain that you feel they have all been punished enough and they may now go out to play except the children caught talking. This way you have been seen to be strict and fair and they will love you for it.

All this may seem a little on the negative side and carried out in this way it would be. Many teachers would prefer to offer rewards for good behaviour:
'If you walk to the hall quietly, we will watch TV.'
rather than,
'If anyone talks on the way to the hall you will not watch TV.'

Children respond well to rewards (which you were going to do anyway) and to positive encouragement. If you tell a class that they are the naughtiest children you have ever met and all your previous classes were so much better than them, they will go out of their way to prove you right. If you tell them that you are disappointed in them because:

'The best class in the school doesn't act like that.'

or:

'Show me how the best class in the school walks to assembly.'

They will respond in a more positive manner.

Using Your Voice

Your voice will also create the right/wrong impression. When one is nervous the voice tends to go higher. Try to pitch your voice lower than you would normally speak to counteract this. When giving commands be forceful but polite. Put 'please' and 'thank you' at the end of instructions:

John, open the door .... thank you.

Open your books at page four, please.

Always repeat instructions at least twice, perhaps using different words. That will extend their vocabulary as well!

Make your voice work for you. Children will respond to the tone of voice as well as to the content of what you are saying. Vary the tone of voice to suit the occasion. Yelling and screaming at a class does not work. It loses your respect (someone yelling is actually quite funny) and they will only become noisier. I'm afraid that the old maxim is true 'Noisy teachers make noisy classes'. However, a good yell and losing of temper (acted or real) from a teacher who normally shows remarkable self-control can be a very salutary experience for a class, but use it with care.

If you speak in normal tones to the children they will quieten down to listen to you. Try getting their attention with a fairly loud voice and then dropping the volume of your voice until you are happy with it. Believe it or not you can actually have the whole class straining to hear your every whisper using this method. A variation of this is to speak to the class quietly so that they have to quieten down to hear you. Of course this means that the first few minutes of what you say can't be really important because it will take them that long to realise that you are speaking. But first you have to get their attention. Most teachers will stand in front of the class, raise their voice (planning to drop it later) and say something to gain the children's attention. When all is quiet and attentive then she will continue with her instructions. The first part of what she says has to be something which is useful only as an attention grabber. You will find that this may become your catch-phrase. Examples are:

Right...

Thank you, children.....

Okay, everybody....

Class four....

Punishments

When a child breaks a rule or behaves badly then you may feel you wish to punish him so that he does not do it again. Punishments should never be given out of vindictiveness or spite. I would also add out of anger but teachers are only human and we all have off-days.

The important thing about punishments is that they should be seen to be fair. I agree with Gilbert and Sullivan's Mikado that the punishment should fit the crime. Bearing this in mind it is usually simple to think of a suitable punishment:

misdemeanour	punishment
not working hard enough	stay in to get work finished
vandalism	clearing up damage
ill-treating another's property	paying for a replacement or writing note of apology to parent
any anti-social behaviour	sitting alone

The problem comes with the more serious crimes; stealing, fighting, swearing, serious acts of vandalism etc. Do not be proud, send the child to a senior member of staff. This will at least cause the rest of the class to recognise the seriousness of the crime. Be very dramatic when you do so. Be totally appalled at their behaviour, emphasise its seriousness and march the culprit to the member of staff (or send for them). This is not a sign of failure of your discipline. Most senior teachers will happily back you up and use their status to show the children that the particular form of behaviour will have serious consequences. It won't do your discipline any harm either, if the children know that if they misbehave they could be sent to Mrs Z.

Rewards

As I have already mentioned, most teachers would prefer to use rewards to elicit the kind of behaviour they want than punishments to punish poor behaviour. Rewards take many forms; the most common being the teacher's approbation. This results in the irritating stream of traffic wanting to know 'Is this all right, Miss?'. However, sometimes you might wish to issue a more positive reward. Here are some ideas:

House Points

The children are in 'houses', either within a class, year, or within the whole school. If a child pleases a teacher for any reason (work, behaviour, improvement etc.) the child is given a house point. At the end of the week/half-term/term/year the house points are added up and the winning house has its coloured ribbon put around a cup/shield. Other things such as Sports Day may involve the children's houses. Some teachers have block graphs on the wall showing who has earned house points for their house.

Sticker/Stars/Sweets/Smiley Faces

This is an instant reward, usually used by individual class teachers. Super Stickers market some excellent stickers at a reasonable price. Their address is:

Super Stickers, 14, Norton Street, Knighton, Powys. LD71ET

Stars can be bought at any good stationers, and sweets usually take the form of smarties, chocolate buttons or small boiled sweets. If the reward is a sweet I usually put 'I CB' (one chocolate button) in the child's book so that he has a record of his reward. Children like stickers for this reason. The stickers can also be made into badges. This works particularly well for the social stickers.

Merit Book

This is either for the school or an individual class. The child's name is entered and at the end of the week/term the children's names are read out. Some schools combine this with house points and automatically give the child a large number of house points if their name is entered in the merit book.

Cups/Shields

At the end of the year some schools give cups/shields to children. Most schools will give cups for effort/improvement as well as achievement.

End of Week Rewards

This is a reward given to a child for effort or improvement during that week. Most teachers will try to make sure that every child receives this reward at least once in the year.

If a child does a particularly good piece of work it can give great pleasure if it is shared in some way with the rest of the school. This can be as simple as sending the child to the Headteacher with his work (Heads like to think they are there for the good things in life as well as the discipline problems!), or showing it to the school in an assembly or displaying it in some special place.

The promise of a reward will work well with most children, but children will tend to see rewards in terms of achievement. It may need to be carefully explained that rewards are 'for doing your best' and in achievement terms one child's best may be very different from another. If this is not done children may perceive your rewards as being unfair.

Dealing With Behavioural Problems

You may have in your class a child who is persistently naughty and no amount of punishments, sending to Headteacher or even parental wrath seems to have any effect. When this situation occurs in most cases (there are always exceptions) there is a reason for the child's behaviour. For a few days keep a diary of when he is naughty and what he did. You may find there is a pattern to his behaviour which you have overlooked and which may give you a clue as to its cause. Here is a list of areas to investigate:

Physical

Is the child physically healthy? Can he see/hear properly? Does he complain of constant sickness or headaches which may be symptoms of an underlying, more serious, problem? Is he getting enough to eat or enough sleep? Is he dressed suitably for the weather? Any of these may affect a child adversely which would result in a lack of concentration and a potential behaviour problem.

The Family

Arrange an interview with his parents and find out if there are problems at home which may be affecting the child emotionally. Watch out for signs of child abuse. Talk to the children generally about saying no and keeping secrets (there are several excellent books to help you deal with this delicate subject) and see if the child will come to you for help. Contact the Educational Welfare Officer for your school and find out if there is anything on record about the family.

At School

Judicious questioning and a careful watch at playtimes will give any information as to whether the child is having problems with his peers. An interview with parents may enable you to see if the problem is with the school, indeed the problem may even be yourself. If this is so then a quiet chat with the child will usually help to quieten his fears.

Sometimes a child will misbehave because you, the teacher, have misjudged his learning potential, i.e. you have given him work which is much too difficult or far too easy. No-one likes doing something at which they constantly fail. If the child's work is of a poor standard and you have mistakenly believed that this was due to laziness and you are punishing him then he is going to give up, resulting in bad behaviour. Conversely, if you give a very able child work which he can do easily, then he will finish his work and find time to play up.

The Child

Rarely, the child may need professional help. If you feel that the child has problems of this nature ask for him to be seen by your Educational Psychologist. Be warned, it may be months before the child is seen and years before a programme is in operation to help him. If you have the support of the parents, you could ask them to start the same process through their General Practitioner. This is usually quicker.

Once you have established the cause of the child's naughtiness, you are in a position to try to help the child modify his behaviour to that which is more acceptable.

Punishments do not usually work with difficult children. If anything they will make the situation worse and alienate you from the child. Try to get the child to see you as someone who is trying to help him. To do this you must set the child clear targets which, with a little effort, he will be able to achieve. Be lavish with your rewards and praise, make the child feel he is special, not because he is naughty, but because he is good.

To do this it is better to break the day into manageable portions. The length of time chosen will depend on the child. Give the child clear instructions as to what he

must do during that time and if he succeeds then he has a reward of a pleasurable activity or a sweet or sticker etc. Some teachers have a 'Good Book' for the child where they keep a record of the child's behaviour during each session. Poor sessions are not punished. Good sessions are always rewarded. If you can, get the parents to sign the book every night and offer their own rewards as well. As the child's behaviour improves you can begin to lengthen the time of the sessions until the child no longer needs the book.

While the child is under this scheme, do try to help him as much as possible. Protect him from his peers and re-arrange your class so that he has no-one near who is likely to distract him. Give him work that you know he enjoys and help him over troublesome times by sending him on a message or giving him a job to do. If he is naughty in assembly, sit him near you, not as a punishment after he has misbehaved but during every assembly so that he can give out the hymn books or hold your bag for you. Try to stop him getting into trouble before he acts. A good way of doing this is to give him responsibility. While he is involved in a worthwhile, task for you he cannot be annoying other children (well that's the theory anyway!).

Taking Unknown Classes

Your discipline with your own class may be fine but many teachers quail at the thought of taking another class. Supply teachers are admired by all of us. Most children will take advantage of a new teacher, especially if she is not a regular member of staff so if you are ever in that unenviable situation, here are some ideas:

1 Before you meet the class, make sure you know the school routine. Do not rely on the children who will assure you with wide-eyed innocence that playtime is always half an hour long.

2 If possible have with you everything that you need for your lessons or ask for it when you arrive at the school. Do not rely on willing volunteers from the children or you may have to send out search parties after an hour or so, to find them.

3 Treat the children as you treated your own class on the first day. Begin by setting high standards.

4 Bluff your way like mad. Pretend an old friendship with their class teacher or an in-depth knowledge of the school.

5 Unless the class teacher has left clear instructions (or you do know the school very well) do not try to keep their usual routine going. While the children are with you, they are going to do this piece of work your way. This will, however, require much stamina to ignore the loud protests from children who thought they could play upon your ignorance.

6 Stop any potential trouble quickly and severely. Send out any real trouble makers to a regular member of staff.

7 Have plenty of work for them to do, especially plenty of time fillers.

8 If they do their work on paper you do not have to get it marked in time for the end of the day. No teacher likes to return to unmarked work in her children's books. Also the work is likely to be sub-standard anyway, and this way no-one will know but you.

9 Unless you are very confident, do not let the children work in groups or pairs. Then they have no opportunity to plot anything.

10 If you do need the help of an individual child (say, for giving out something) do not ask for volunteers, just choose someone who looks harmless. Volunteers can have ulterior motives.

Noise

The amount of noise your class generates depends on you in two respects. Firstly how noisy you are yourself; if you yell and scream the children will follow your example. Secondly, the noise level you are prepared to tolerate. This varies from teacher to teacher and is no indication of discipline. The noise level will also vary with the age of the children and what they are doing. That being said, an undisciplined class will tend to be noisy because the teacher is unable to control the noise level. So here are some ideas for when you are faced with a rowdy class who appear to be taking no notice of you:

1 Start off every lesson in a controlled way. Do not let children wander round the classroom, go to their bags, write the date or talk while you are talking to them. When the time comes for them to begin their work they will be quiet from the start.

2 When faced with inattention do not ask for quiet in general terms, pick on individual children. If you do not know their names, make up a suitable name:
   'Hey, Fred at the back, stop talking.'
   'Hey you, with the blue jumper, I said put your pens down.'

3 Give the children chance to quieten down. Standing and waiting at the front of the class may have the desired effect on its own, but if it doesn't, do give them a few minutes for what you have said to sink in.

4 If the noise level begins to rise tell them they are too noisy and things should quieten down.

5 If they begin to get noisy again pick out, and if necessary move, a few likely individuals.

6 If the noise level continues to rise begin to threaten with forfeiture of playtime or PE (to make up for the time they are obviously wasting by talking now). You can threaten this generally or specifically to a few troublemakers.

7 If the noise really does get out of control you can risk all by telling the class they will now work in silence. Anyone who talks will miss their playtime/PE. If you are going to use this it is better to set a time limit of five or, at most, ten minutes as children find this very difficult. The nicest child in the class with probably forget first and ask his friend for a rubber. After the period of silence you should find the class works more quietly.

8 A variation on 7 is to tell the children they are going to work in silence and lose one minute of playtime for everyone that talks. After they have lost five minutes they should have the message.

Individual Problems (or Problem Individuals)

Usually there are only one or two children in the class who will cause you discipline problems. Once you have demonstrated your authority to these, the rest of the class should pose no problems. It will not take you long to work out who these children are. They will be looking for any sign of perceived weakness in yourself. They will not consider you compassionate because you change your mind and let them off their well-deserved punishment with a heart-to-heart talk; they will see it as a sign of their cleverness.

When you take over the class these are the children who will test you. They may be cheeky, answer you back, act the class clown or be outright defiant. In all these incidents they are trying you out. They want to know what you are going to do. If you do nothing or become upset, they will have no respect for you at all and you will be unable to control them.

These children can make a teacher's life a nightmare, so it is important that you show them who is boss from the very start. How you deal with each situation depends to a certain extent on your own personality but there are a few golden rules:

1 You have to show the child who is boss without a direct confrontation. The best way to do this is to ridicule him. For this you need to have a quicker sense of humour than him. Give him a quick answer back and before he has time to reply get the class working.

2 Don't put yourself in a position where the child can defy you outright. He won't obey you just because you are the teacher so you have to make him do what you want because he wants to do it to. This can be by (supposed) reward or by putting him in a position whereby he would look foolish in front of his classmates. Let's say you wish to move a child off a table where he has been misbehaving, to another table with quieter well-behaved children.

'Your work is so good I think you had better move off this table where these children are disturbing you [sarcasm is completely lost on children] and come onto this table.'

Once you have the children laughing at the trouble maker, you have scored on two counts. Firstly, he has to obey your wishes or appear a spoil-sport and secondly, you have made him the centre of attention and you are not cross with him or punishing him. You are on his side and, hopefully, he will be on yours. Once you get a child like this on your side, it is a very special relationship and well worth the effort.

3 Give the child responsibility. If he fails to fulfil it properly, he is again open to ridicule. You will find that children like this thrive on being the centre of attention. Make them the centre of attention in some other way and they will stop playing you up. A position of responsibility does this nicely. Your problem may be to stop him being over zealous!

Class Problems

One of the most awkward discipline problems is when something has happened and you know that the culprit is a member of a group of children, usually a class. How do you find the culprit? If the incident is something small, such as a missing pair of scissors or a broken ruler you could punish the whole group. But if it is something more serious you will need to find out exactly who the culprit was. Children are only human and if they know that they are in for serious trouble, why should they own up? Your task is to then make it easy for them to own up so that they feel they will be gaining something — such as clemency. Many teachers will treat a child more leniently if he owns up and make sure that the children know this. If you already have this relationship with your children they are more likely to trust you when it comes to owning up over major issues.

The child's peers are probably horrified by the crime so you have to protect the culprit from them as well. You can do this in two ways. Indicate to the class that you feel sure that the culprit is now feeling very sorry for what he has done and that we all make mistakes. You are sure that what has happened was not the normal behaviour of the person involved and that they gave way to temptation . . . etc . . . etc. Offer the culprit the opportunity to own up/make amends in private. Promise them that the rest of the class need never know who it was that did the dastardly deed.

Bluff your class into thinking that you have other ways of finding out who did it. Threaten to take the matter to the appropriate authority to make it clear that it would be better if the person owned up now.

If none of these work then you either have a hardened criminal in your class or the child responsible is away!

Tale-telling

Not many of us like tell-tales. They are usually viewed as children trying to curry favour with the teacher by reporting the small misdemeanours of other children. Not surprisingly the other children do not like them either. However, another way of viewing a tell-tale is that the child has seen something that he knows is wrong but the child that has done it has not been punished. The child has come to you to ascertain that what he thought was wrong is wrong. In other words the child is trying to make sense of his world and needs reassurance that his judgement over what is acceptable and unacceptable behaviour is correct. Whatever the reason, most teachers will not punish children on the word of a tell-tale. But they will probably keep an eye on the child and try to catch him misbehaving for themselves!

Children often become confused over when it is tale-telling and when it is their moral duty to report a serious crime to the teacher. Much of this will depend on their relationship with their teacher.

If a serious misdemeanour has been reported, it is still not wise to punish on the word of the reporter alone. Ask for other witnesses to the event. Listen to each of their stories and then send for the culprit. Hear his story, (without interruption from the outraged witnesses) and ask the culprit if he has anyone to back up his story (ignore the testimony of close friends and younger, smaller children for obvious reasons). Having heard all of the witnesses you will probably have a good idea of what really happened. If the culprit still flatly denies being involved, depending on the known characters of the children, you may have to call his bluff. Help him out with a more lenient view of the incident and you may get him to confess that he was partially to blame.

Organising Reading

No-one can really over-emphasise the importance of the skill of reading in our everyday lives and much has been written about the way we acquire that skill. It is not the purpose of this book to advocate specific teaching methods in the teaching of reading but to help with the organisation of that teaching.

Reading is involved in almost every aspect of the curriculum, a fact which is easily forgotten. Often children fail to do a task set from a book, not because they are unable to perform the task, but simply because the text of the book is beyond the level of their reading skill.

Many children (and parents) think of progress in reading in terms of the child's reading book. Most teachers will have come across the question, 'He read *War and Peace* in the holidays so why is he only on reading book four?'. It is tempting to push a child on through the reading levels of an appropriate scheme but if you do so you are recognising only one skill — that of decoding.

Your teaching and classroom should reflect the importance of reading and there are many ways in which to do this.

Promoting Reading

Looking around the classroom there are many ways in which we encourage children to read. We have books readily available. We have bright, attractive displays, often with captions which took hours to prepare. We display children's written work or even make it into a book.

Fine. Now look again. The books, how old are they? Are they falling to bits? Are the illustrations modern? What condition are they in? Does the subject matter reflect the interests and background of your pupils? Are they clean? Many people (and I am one of them) love books because of their texture and smell as well as for their visual delights. Are you fostering this in your children or are you putting them off with tatty, out-of-date, grimy books simply because you can't bear to throw away the printed word in any shape or form? Re-appraise your stock of reading books and throw away everything that you find distasteful to handle or which have out-of-date illustrations. Most modern reading books respond well to a wipe over with a damp cloth at the end of the summer term. A word of warning — this is a task you have to do yourself, unless you are really short of papier-mâché.

How long have these books been in your classroom? Is it possible to change them termly, or yearly? Has your local library service an arrangement with schools whereby you can borrow and exchange books regularly? If you do this, don't change all the books at once. Change half a dozen or so every two weeks. If there is no such service from your library, can you change your books with a colleague or the school library? Most class libraries are fairly small and it is important to keep the children's interest by changing books regularly if it is possible.

How are your books displayed? Is the bookshelf or display case a suitable height for children? Too low can be as bad as too high and to allow certain children licence to grovel about on the floor is asking for trouble. Are the books easy to take off and to return to the shelf? Too tightly packed and they will not be returned correctly, too loose and they will be in a terrible muddle within ten minutes.

How do you encourage children to notice books? Here are some ways of promoting books in your classroom.

1 Display some books, preferably on a particular theme. Your topic is an obvious choice but other themes could include books of a particular genre or by a particular author, or books relating to the weather or customs of the time of year. If possible display the books open at an interesting page. The W-shaped wire book stands are good for this.

2 Promote one book a week. It could be displayed as shown below.

In the Summer term I ask the children to write the review. I have learnt about many excellent children's books this way.

Read an exciting part of the book to your class to whet their appetites. It helps if you finish reading with a cliff-hanger.

3   Read exciting portions of different books to your class rather than (or as well as) having a class reader.

4   Hold a book-week. A useful book to help you is the *Children's Bookweek Handbook* available from Book Trust, 45, East Hill, London, SW18 2QZ A booklet containing useful practical information *Classroom activities for Bookweeks* is available from Puffin Book Clubs at the address below.

5   Arrange a visit to your local library. Many children are not taken to the library by their parents and may view it as a forbidding place. Hopefully, once they have visited the library with you they will talk their parents into going again.

6   Set a good example yourself. Talk freely about your own reading and try to read all the books you have in your library so that you can discuss them with your children.

7   Give reading an important position in the school day. Don't let it be a task set when other work is finished. Have a regular period in the day when everyone sits and reads silently (the whole school if possible). The teacher should be reading as well (it's a wonderful introduction to the afternoon and very tempting to extend the time if you are feeling fragile or have a good book!). The children should have two books for 'silent reading'. I usually let them have their reading book and a totally free choice of book. This means that they have structured reading but they may also be extending themselves and reading for pleasure from a book which particularly interests them. No-one changes their book during silent reading. If you finish one book you read the other.

The duration of silent reading will vary with the age and ability of your class. Infants gain most from having five minutes sitting quietly, learning how to handle a book correctly, looking at picture books. With older children you can extend the time over the course of the year from ten minutes to however long you can spare.

8   Run a school bookshop or bookclub. The two main organisations which run bookclubs for schools are

Puffin Bookclubs, Penguin Books, 27, Wrights Lane, London, W8 5TZ

Scholastic Publications Ltd., Westfield Road, Leamington Spa, Warwickshire, CV33 0BR

Some major bookshops also operate a bookclub for children on an individual or group basis. Your local library should be able to give you details of any that operate in your area. Usually the company will send a leaflet at regular intervals for the child to take home. The leaflet gives details and prices of books the club is offering, sometimes at a discount on shop prices. Parents send in their money and order to school who send off the total order to the company. The school profits by receiving a percentage of the amount sold or free books.

9 Ask the children to bring in and read to the rest of the class sections from their favourite book.

Now look at your displays from a child's point of view i.e. from a child's desk and at a child's height. You may find that your interest is mainly centred around the back walls of the classroom — where you and visitors have to look. But children will probably be looking forward to where you have your desk — by the chalkboard (or heater). Your captions may be too small to be read from the middle of the room or too high to be read from close by. Teachers in the temporary, demountable classrooms have a particular problem because their display space is above the level of the children's coat hooks. This means that you need mountaineering equipment whenever you wish to change your displays and that they are too high for the children to browse through and read them. Admit defeat and put all reading matter at the bottom of such displays, with diagrams and pictures at the top.

Do you allow children time to read your displays? Or if they leave their place do you accuse them of time-wasting?

Are the children being given enough variety of reading material? Often reading material in classrooms is limited to fiction books. Have you provided non-fiction books, catalogues, newspapers, magazines, comics, games, work by the children

themselves or other children? Don't forget that text can be presented in many different ways. It can be shown on the computer screen or printed by the printer. It can be typed or handwritten. All of these can be in a variety of styles.

Another way of indicating the importance of reading is to set aside a part of the classroom solely for that activity — a 'Reading Corner'. Most teachers furnish their Reading Corner informally with carpeting, soft seating and even a plant or two. In the Reading Corner a child can lose himself in a book away from the hustle and bustle of the rest of the class. Children enjoy being in the Reading Corner and will often ask to go there.

Organising Reading Books

In most schools reading books are organised in terms of their level of difficulty. In some schools these levels may be designated by the reading scheme that the school has chosen to use. However, most schools prefer to use a variety of reading schemes, drawing on the strengths of each and matching them to the needs and interests of each particular child. If a school is using two or three, or perhaps even more schemes there is a need for the school to organise its reading resources so that books of a similar difficulty are grouped together. There are three main ways of doing this.

1 Experience

As the teacher becomes familiar with the books she will know that if a child can cope with *Ginn Level 7* he can cope with *Wide Range Book 1*. To become more organised this does mean that someone has to identify all the books of a similar level of difficulty for other, less experienced, teachers. This is an extremely time-consuming task and based on the value-judgement of one teacher (even if she does use a readability test). Fortunately a comparison of the major reading schemes has already been undertaken by three companies.

2 The Ginn System

The Ginn publishing company were one of the first companies to publish a reading scheme which also encompassed language development. The scheme is based on thirteen levels, each with its own colour.

Level	Colour	Reading Age
1	red	pre-reading
2	yellow	5 yrs
3	turquoise	5–6 yrs
4	lime	6 yrs
5	purple	6–7 yrs
6	orange	7 yrs
7	pink	7–8 yrs
8	navy	8 yrs
9	green	8–9 yrs
10	cerise	9–10 yrs
11	rust	10–11 yrs
12	sage	11–12 yrs
13	brown	12–13 yrs

Ginn also publish a *Comparative Reading Chart* which shows where books from the other major reading schemes fit into the Ginn levels. They also sell labels coloured to correspond with the colours of the reading scheme levels so that their levels can be used for all books in the school.

3 The 'Moon System'

The Centre for the Teaching of Reading at the University of Reading publishes a list of books grouped in stages for individualised reading. There are fourteen stages with suggested colour codings for each stage. Even if you do n   wish to adopt the individualised approach to learning, the book is a useful resource for integrating reading schemes.

Individualised Reading Bernice and Cliff Moon, Centre for the Teaching of Reading, School of Education, University of Reading, Berkshire.

4 National Association for Remedial Education

This association publishes much useful resource material for teachers. One of their publications is *An A-Z list of Reading Books* by E. J. Atkinson and C. W. Gains, edited by Roy Edwards. This useful book catalogues reading books in lists of interest and readability. Further details are available from NARE Publications, 2, Lichfield Road, Stafford, ST17 4JX.

Once you have the labels and the book or chart it is relatively easy to grade all the reading books in your school according to either of the last three systems. But there are still some problems. In practice many teachers have found that some of the comparisons are not quite accurate and books may have to be moved up or down a level. Sometimes the degree of difficulty within a level can be so great that you still have to guide children through the easier books on the level until they are confident enough to face the more difficult. You may have books which are not compared under either system. You will then have to use your own judgement or do a readability test. Despite the expertise and hard work that has gone into published systems, do not undervalue your own experience and expertise. You know your children and if you know that they will find something particularly easy or difficult, then trust your own judgement, using the books and chart as a guide, not a rule.

Readability Testing

A readability test gives a rough guide as to the level of skill needed to read a book. It is a useful test to know when you have a book which does not fit into the *Ginn* or *Moon* systems of grading books.

A simple method of testing the readability of a book is to take three passages, each of ten sentences. Count the number of words with three or more syllables. Call this number 'S'. The reading age can then be worked out using the following formula.

$$\text{Reading Age} = \frac{S}{7} + 8$$

For example if you find 50 words of three or more syllables from your three passages.

$$\text{Reading Age} = \frac{S}{7} + 8$$

$$\text{Reading Age} = \frac{50}{7} + 8$$

$$\text{Reading Age} = 7 + 8$$
$$\text{Reading Age} = 15 \text{ yrs}$$

Storing Reading Books

Once the books have been graded they need to be easily accessible for both teachers and children. The ideal situation is that all the books you need are kept in the classroom but because many classes may been needing books on the same level, the books are usually kept in a central area. It is not really suitable to have reading books stored in one classroom as children need to feel free to change their books as they are needed. Young children need help in finding the correct book and this can be very disruptive for the poor teacher who houses the school's reading resources.

Even with a central resource area, many teachers like to keep a small number of reading books in their classrooms. Infant teachers may wish to have all the early levels in their room as their children change their books so frequently. Young children find it difficult to return books to shelves so many infant teachers keep their books in baskets or boxes clearly labelled with the level colour.

Juniors can usually cope with returning books to shelves but it helps to label the shelf with the appropriate colour/number. It also helps the children if you put the easier levels on the lower shelves and the harder levels on a higher shelf as the younger (smaller) children will need the easier books.

Reading Records

In order to monitor a child's progress and ensure some form of continuity and progression between classes some form of record is kept of the child's progress in reading. The school may have its own reading records which you may have to complete or you may have to make your own. You may also wish to keep your own records to supplement those required by the school or Education Authority. There are many ways of keeping a record of a child's reading and you may already have found one which works for you. If not, here are some ideas.

1 The Exercise Book

Keep an exercise book for each child and keep a record of the date, the book and page number that the child is reading. Comments can be written in the book by adults who listen to the child read and this can be a valuable link between home and school.

   The problems with this widely used method is that it is not easy to see at a glance which books the child has read. The book can become easily lost between home and school and the teacher may wish to record something which may distress the parent.

2 The Reading Card

This is similar to the exercise book. The child is given a large piece of card which is usually used as a book mark. On the card is recorded the child's book and page number and any difficulties.

   This is a useful way of informally recording a child's progression through the reading scheme but as it does not give any details of the child's strengths and weaknesses it should really be used along with another form of record keeping.

3 The Record Book

With this method the teacher has a Reading Record Book, allowing a few pages for each child. In the book she keeps a record of the child's progress and problems and, perhaps, his book.

This method has to be used with either numbers 1 or 2 because the other adults listening to the child read will not know which page the child has reached. Children never know whereabouts in a book they have reached. If they have remembered, it never fails to amaze me how they always stop reading at the foot of a page.

4 The Record Sheet

A sheet is produced listing the school reading books. When a child has read a particular book it is crossed off in some way. This is a very easy way of keeping track of what a child has read and ensuring progression through the school. This is made clearer if different colours are used for different years. The record sheet can be used to show which book the child is currently reading by using a symbol which is crossed out when the book has been finished.

This method only lists the books that the child has read. There is no record of the other aspects of reading. However the back of the sheet could be used to record other details of the child's progress.

5 A Tick Sheet

This is a pre-prepared sheet of the skills involved in learning to read. When the teacher feels that the child has learnt the skill, it is 'ticked-off'. It is a useful checklist to show what has been covered.

Again this sheet does not really record the individual problems experienced by a child. You must be careful not to tick something just because it has been taught — it does not necessarily mean it has been learnt.

Listening to Children Read

Many people confuse the teaching of reading with listening to a child read. The act of listening to reading has many educational benefits. It is a time when the child has adult attention all to himself and this can be very important in building a useful working relationship between teacher and child. However the teacher must use the time to monitor and assess the child's reading ability so that she can plan a teaching programme suitable for the continuing development of the child's reading skills.

When listening to a child read the following may be useful:

1 Make sure that the child is at ease and comfortable. The child (and teacher) should both enjoy the shared experience.

2 The child should not learn to view reading to the teacher as a form of test. If you need to make notes, try to do this after the child has returned to their place. It is not pleasant to have someone scribbling while you are trying to do your best.

3 Try to give the child your undivided attention. The other children can see you in between readers.

4 Try to keep a record of the child's errors so that you can help him to overcome problems later.

5 Don't be too quick to prompt. Offer assistance after the child has had an attempt at the unknown word.

6 Encourage a variety of strategies for decoding unknown words:

    ▷ **context clues** — i.e. read the whole sentence and guess the missing word

    ▷ **visual clues**   — the illustrations may give a clue to the unknown word

    ▷ **phonic clues** — get the child to 'sound the word out'

7 Some teachers record, on the child's book mark, words that proved difficult, so that they can be revised whenever the child reads to an adult. If the child reads the word correctly on three separate occasions then the word is crossed off as having been learnt.

8 How often you listen to readers is largely a matter of time and personal preference. Most people would agree that younger children need to be heard more frequently as that is probably the only time they actually 'read'. Older children will (hopefully) be reading on their own but still need to be heard regularly to monitor their progress.

9 Often teachers forget that reading aloud is a different skill to reading silently. Try to encourage expression and a suitable pace. If the child is expressionless get him to read the passage after you and copy the modulations of your voice.

10 Ask the child questions about what he has just read. Not only questions to check comprehension, but ask him what could happen next, whether he likes the book and ask him to give reasons for his answers.

Parents Listening to Readers

Many parents volunteer their services to help in the classroom and one way in which they can be useful is in hearing children read. Most parents will try to help their child at home by listening to him read regularly. It must be stressed that useful as this help is, to achieve the maximum benefit the parent must be able to support the work of the class teacher. Clear guidance is necessary or over-enthusiastic help can confuse a child.

Many of the points covered in teachers listening to children read will also apply to parents with the addition of:

1 Show the parent your method of recording which children you have heard read. If you have several parents helping this can prove to be a muddle. An idea is to have a register written on squared paper and each parent fills in the child's square for that week with a pen stroke.

So the register could look like this:

John Smith ⊠ ◹ Heard by teacher.

Ann Pupil ⊠ ◺ Heard by parent 1.

Susan Atkins ◹ ⊟ Heard by parent 2

George Jones ⊠

2 Your method of recording the child's place in the book should be clearly explained. Some teachers like to hear the whole book themselves before they allow the child to change it. Other teachers ask that the parent records the numbers of the pages read and will not ask the child to repeat them.

3 If you are recording unknown words, this system needs to be explained.

4 If you wish to encourage the parent to write comments on the child's reading, this also needs to be explained.

5   You must also make clear your strategies for dealing with unknown words. Most parents will prompt too quickly and the child will pause, waiting for the prompt without making any effort to work out the word for himself.

Group Reading

This is now largely unfashionable because it did not allow for the individuality of children and because buying a set of a single book is very expensive. However, many teachers feel that there is a place for group reading not least because children enjoy it and anything which gets them enjoying reading has to be a good thing!

There are various ways of tackling group reading. If you are worried that it may cause chaos here are some that have been tried and tested.

1   The children read a sentence of the book each, round the class.

   This is very stilted if you have poor readers but less boring than *2* if you have good readers. It also teaches what is and is not a sentence!

2   The children read a paragraph each.

   The problem is that paragraphs can vary enormously in length and you can guarantee your poorest reader is going to read three quarters of a page and your best reader two sentences.

3   The children read a page each.

   Alright in theory but very boring for the child who has to read last.

4   You (or a competent reader) read the narrative, the other children read the speech as if it were a play.

5   You buy a set of plays (e.g. the *Take Part* series, Puffin) and give the children a part according to their reading ability. The children then form into their groups and read their plays at the same time.

   Not a quiet lesson this, but I have not yet had a class that did not thoroughly enjoy it.

   If you wish the whole class to read a play, give each of the children a part (major parts can be split). It helps to keep the play moving if you read the stage directions.

Reading to Children

The best advice I can offer for this is to tape yourself. It is a salutary experience. Children love being read to (probably because you're doing all the work) but often we lose their interest because we read badly.

Before you begin, try to make sure that they are comfortable. Most younger children are happy sitting on a carpeted floor. If the children are not used to sitting and doing nothing let them pursue a quiet activity — sewing or colouring are ideal. On no account does anyone talk or leave their place. This may seem a radical idea but how many adults listen to the radio or hi-fi and do nothing? Better that they are occupied positively than left to their own devices.

Remind them of the story so far and begin by reading a few sentences from the previous session to recapture the mood.

When you are reading look up frequently to gauge the reaction of your audience and to make sure they are behaving themselves.

Read slowly and with expression. Try to give different characters different voices. The bigger fool you make of yourself the more alive your reading will be.

Always leave the story at a cliff hanger. There is nothing so pleasurable than the 'Oooooohhhhhh' when you close the book for the end of storytime.

You will know when a book isn't going down well. Even if it does fit in perfectly with your topic or it was your favourite book when you were eight, change it for another.

Reading Tests

Many schools and teachers test their children regularly in order to ascertain the children's progress in reading. Mostly the test will verify what the teacher already believes about the child's ability or progress but, occasionally, the test indicates something that the teacher has not realised. Standardised tests are also useful to the teacher because they give some indication of how the reading ability of the child compares with other children in his age-group.

It must be remembered that nothing replaces the experience of the teacher and if you feel that a child has done unusually well or poorly on a standardised test, look for an explanation.

Most reading tests will give you a reading age. Be careful when you compare reading ages from one test to another as some list the ages in years and months i.e. '7yrs 3mths' and some in decimal form '7.3'. Make sure you know whether the .3 is three tenths or three months. The reading age really gives you an idea of the child's ability to decode a word, sentence or passage. It gives you no idea of the child's skill level in other areas of reading or of his level of comprehension.

Some tests are designed to give the comprehension age as well as the reading age. Ideally the reading age and comprehension age should be equal but in practice most children are better at decoding than understanding what they are reading. At the lower junior age-range parents often complain that their children are not making the speedy progress through the reading scheme that they did in their infant class. This is usually because the children are now reading to improve their understanding, having mastered most of the necessary decoding skills.

A third category of tests are diagnostic in that they are a series of tests given to a child in order to see if he can cope with the skills necessary for learning to read e.g. left to right orientation, basic sight vocabulary, phonic skills. Sometimes these tests are given to a child who is not making progress in reading in order to establish on which skill the teacher needs to concentrate.

It can be seen that when you give a reading test and when you are interpreting the results you have to be clear as to exactly what the test was testing. You must also allow for the human factor in testing. Some teachers will be more generous in allowing mistakes than others. It is preferable that all the children are tested by the same person for truly accurate results.

Children know when they are being tested and often want to know their results. It is impossible to tell them their true results but you can give them a rough comparison with their last test i.e. much better, a little better, better, the same, worse, much worse. If the child has not made the progress you expected through laziness you may like to turn this situation to your advantage in that everyone except him will be receiving your praise and be patting themselves on the back. How you treat this situation will depend on the temperament of the child.

Record Keeping and Testing

Keeping Records

Keeping records is probably one of the most irksome but necessary parts of the task of teaching. Most schools will insist upon some form of record keeping and many teachers keep their own records. Without some form of record it is impossible to know what skills the children have already covered, their level of ability and any other useful information the previous class teacher feels you need to know — don't sit Johnny next to Fred or what to do if Isabel has an asthma attack.

Records are important to ensure that you build up the foundation laid down by the child's previous teachers. This does not mean that there is not scope for your own abilities or interests but in certain curriculum areas it means that the child does not repeat work he has already satisfactorily mastered in an earlier class. This is particularly important with the introduction of the National Curriculum where it is necessary to know which attainment targets the child has met and how satisfactorily he has mastered them. Also adequate records must be kept to show that the National Curriculum is being covered properly.

Records help with continuity and they come in three main types:

Official

This is the child's school record which is passed from school to school and has to be kept. The format is different for each education authority but the basic information is the same. They want to know about the child's home background i.e. name and address of parent(s), position in family, name of family doctor etc.

In this record will also be information about any official meetings with the parents and any letters sent to the parents or education authority about the child. It will also contain any medical or psychological reports on the child and records of the child's work (often in the form of a copy of his report) and the results of any standardised tests.

It may be that eventually this record will also contain a description of the child's level of attainment in all areas of the National Curriculum.

Parents now have the right to view their child's school record.

School

These are records that your Headteacher asks you to keep. In some schools they may be legion, in other schools non-existent. Usually they are kept for the main subject areas of Maths, English (reading) and Science. Often they take the form of a tick sheet which really only shows that you have covered the work, not that the child has grasped the skill or concept concerned. A more useful variation of the tick sheet is where a box is filled as follows:

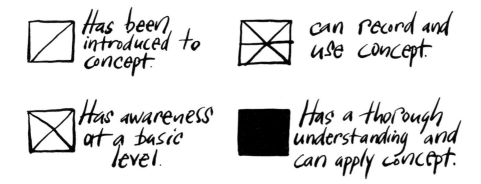

If different colours are used for different years then the child's progress is clear.

Many schools are now basing their record keeping on the attainment targets of the National Curriculum. The above method is equally useful for this because it does give some indication of how well the child understands the concept involved. Teachers may feel more secure using the National Curriculum as a basis for the record keeping as it does help them to see which areas of the National Curriculum they have still to cover with their children.

Personal

You may wish to keep your own records of your children's progress. A good idea (if you have the self-discipline) is to have a page in your record book for each child. When something important happens involving that child, you make of note of it with the date. This does make writing the child's report easier at the end of the year. It also provides you with times and dates of misdemeanours which may fall into a discernible pattern which you may not have noticed otherwise.

Many teachers feel the need to keep a record of the children's marks for tests (standardised or otherwise) or for pieces of work. They will mentally grade the work A — E or give a mark out of ten. I must stress that the child has no idea of this system and will have his work returned with suitably constructive comments. The advantage of this is that you do have a precise record of the standard of every child's work in whichever areas you wish to keep records. It is also ammunition for Parents Evening, should you need it. The disadvantage is that it is extremely time consuming to mark books and keep records this way and you may feel that your time could be better spent. You may also find that you tend to 'label' children more using this system. Many teachers also feel that a row of marks of this nature does not really tell you very much about the strengths and problems the child may have and would prefer to trust their own knowledge of the child.

Keeping records of standardised tests can be more helpful as one can see how the child has progressed in relation to the 'norm'. This can be a salutary experience if you felt that a child was making good progress in reading and yet his score has not increased. In looking for a reason why, you may find a problem of which you were unaware. However all standardised tests should be judged in the light of their

particular strengths and weaknesses and if there is a great discrepancy between your knowledge of the child and his score, check his health, the children he was sitting near during the test — and trust your own judgement!

Testing

On a very simple level we test children to find out what they know but this is not terribly helpful to the class teacher other than as a starting point for teaching. More useful are tests which show which skills a child has acquired and which areas need more work — such as a group of tests for reading readiness. Other tests which are useful for the class teacher are tests which show why a child has a particular problem with something — diagnostic tests.

The range of tests which have been developed recently test the child's cognitive development: the strategies he has for solving problems. In order to cope with this type of testing the child must have had a broad range of experiences and to be able to apply the knowledge gained to challenging circumstances.

Bearing in mind that nothing can replace the teacher's knowledge and experience of the child, let us look at the types of test available for the class teacher.

Tests of Knowledge

In this type of test the child is asked a question to which there is only one answer:

Spell 'patient'
What is the capital of France?
Re-write the passage putting in all the full-stops and capital letters

Many teachers use this type of test as part of their teaching — spelling is a good example of this, or as a guide to how much the children have learnt from a specific piece of work, for example a topic. It can be also used as a time filler or a game. Children love facts; the more bizarre the better and enjoy quiz-type games which enable them to show off this knowledge.

IQ Tests

IQ (Intelligence Quotient) tests were very popular a few years ago until modern research made us aware of the more complex relationship between learning and intelligence, and that a high score on an IQ test does not necessarily mean all learning skills will be easily acquired.

However, it is sometimes useful to have a rough guide to a child's intellectual ability if you suspect that you have a child with exceptional abilities or that you have a child who is not making the progress you feel he should be making.

One of the easiest tests to administer to give you a guide to the child's IQ is the *Goodenough Test*.

The Goodenough Draw-a-Man Test

Task
The child is required to draw a picture of a man or woman.

Materials
Pencil and paper.

Method
The child is given the paper and pencil and asked to draw the best picture of a man or woman that he can.

Scoring
Score one mark for each of the following items in the drawing:

1 Head present.

2 Legs present.

3 Arms present.

4 Trunk present.

5 Length of trunk greater than breadth but not a mere line.

6 Shoulders shown (not merely rectangular or elliptical).

7 Both arms and legs attached to trunk.

8 Legs attached to trunk. Arms attached at correct point. (Full face — exact: profile not at back, neck or too low.)

9 Neck present.

10 Outline of neck continuous with that of head, trunk or of both.

11 Eyes present (one or two).

12 Nose present.

13 Mouth present.

14 Both nose and mouth two-dimensional, two lips shown not a straight line, dot or circle; a triangle is accepted. (In profile, either lips modelled or line continuous.)

15 Nostrils indicated.

16 Hair shown.

17 Hair present on more than circumference of head and non-transparent. Method of representation better than a scribble.

18 Clothing present. (Buttons count.)

19 Two articles of clothing present (excluding buttons). Non-transparent.

20 Entire drawing free from transparencies when both sleeves and trousers shown.

21 Four or more articles of clothing definitely indicated (e.g. hat, cap, shirt, collar, tie, belt, braces, trousers, shoes — with some detail apart from heel).

22 Costume complete. All essentials recognisable without incongruities (be strict).

23 Fingers shown — any indication. Both hands, but if only one arm, then one hand enough.

24 Correct number of fingers shown.

25 Opposition (clear differentiation) of thumb shown.

26 Fingers shown in two dimensions. Length greater than breadth and total angle not greater than 180 degrees.

27 Hand shown as distinct from fingers/arms.

28 Arm joint shown — either elbow, shoulder or both. It must show a distinct bend.

29 Leg joint shown — either knee, hip or both. It must show a distinct bend.

30 Head shown in correct proportion (one-half to one-tenth the area of the trunk).

31 Arms shown in proportion (equal or longer than trunk, not wider, shorter than knee).

32 Legs shown in proportion (one to two times the length of the trunk, not wider).

33 Feet shown in proportion (one-third to one-tenth the length of the leg, two dimensional, not clubbed).

34 Both arms and legs shown two dimensional.

35 Heel shown.

Motor Co-ordination

36 A All lines reasonably firm and meeting.

37 B Be very strict, all lines quite firm and meeting.

38 C Head outline — no irregularities. Better than a primitive circle or ellipse. Lines firm and meeting. Score rigidly.

39 D Trunk outline ditto.

40 E Arms and legs — ditto. Not narrowing at body.

41 Features — ditto. All symmetrical and two-dimensional. In profile, eye at least two-thirds of the way back from the back of the head towards the nose; nose and mouth in proportion with the rest of the head.

42 Ears present.

43 Ears present in correct proportion and position (not circular and showing some detail if shown on profile drawing).

44 Eye detail — brow or lashes shown.

45 Pupil shown.

46 Eye shown in proportion — elongated. (In profile a sector of a circle is acceptable).

47 Glance elongated to the front in profile drawings of the eye.

48 Both chin and forehead shown.

49 Profile drawing with not more than one error (such as bodily transparency, legs not in profile, arms attached to back etc.).

50 Correct profile.

Norms for Determining Age

Points	2	6	10	12	14	18	22	26	30	34	38	42
Mental Age (in years)	3	4	5	5.5	6	7	8	9	10	11	12	13

When comparing results the child's physical age is taken from his last birthday.

This is a very useful test if you wish to have a general idea of the intellectual ability of a child. But as you can see it is rather subjective and it is often helpful to have a drawing marked twice by different teachers. You can then use the average of the two results. As with all tests this is fallible in that some children with learning difficulties in other areas of the curriculum are very talented artists. This is another occasion where your knowledge of the child is important when administering standardised tests.

Diagnostic

These are a series of tests which you give to a child to ascertain why he is not making the progress of which you think he is capable. It could be that he was absent when a certain skill was taught and the lack of this skill is preventing his further progress. These tests will pinpoint exactly where the problem lies and, hopefully, when you have taken some remedial action, the child should continue to make progress according to his age and ability.

An excellent battery of tests is the *Aston Index* published by LDA the address of which can be found in *Appendices* on p149.

Spelling Tests

Not the tests teachers give on a Friday morning, but a standardised test to give a child's 'Spelling Age'. This can be useful if you are worried about a particular child's ability to spell, or you wish to have a rough guide of the spelling ability of a new class in order to group them for the Friday morning tests.

On p149–150 in *Appendices* there is an example of a useful spelling test.

Maths Tests

The more useful of the many maths tests available will give you an idea of the child's weaknesses as well as giving you an idea of how well he is performing compared with the 'norm'. Some tests will give you the child's results as a profile which makes it very easy to see where the child's strengths and weaknesses lie. This makes future planning of the child's work much easier. Some of the major maths schemes have progress tests which link with the work of the scheme.

Non-Verbal Tests

Most tests rely on the child's ability to read and understand what he is required to do. This, in some measure, tests the child's reading rather than his ability to perform the test. To help to overcome this problem tests have been devised where there are no wordy instructions or answers. These tests are particularly appropriate for infants. However they can only really test the child's cognitive abilities and not specific skills.

Reading Tests

These are dealt with in the chapter on *Organising Reading*.

Administering Tests

The objective is for the child to perform to the best of his ability. To do this he needs to be in a non-stressful situation and unable to communicate with other children. These are difficult to achieve.

The way to relieve the stress of tests is for the teacher to be calm and reassuring. I sometimes tell the children that the test tells me how good a job I am doing. If they can't do something then it is my fault because I should have taught them better! This takes the pressure off the individual child.

The other way to relieve pressure is to have a testing situation frequently. In this way the children are not expected to do their best in a new situation.

To prevent communication and copying the children are usually seated at the ends of their desks as far apart as possible. Have a reading book ready for anyone who finishes early and it can also be used to cover up finished work. Pencils and rubbers will also be needed.

Make sure that everyone has been to the toilet before the test begins but be sympathetic to the effect of test nerves! If the test is to be timed strictly, give regular timechecks. Children often waste a lot of time struggling with one answer which means that they did not attempt answers near the end of the test which they could do easily. Tell children to do all the questions they can do easily first and then go back over the questions they need to think about. Children will also need to be told to check their work and to read the question carefully.

Reports

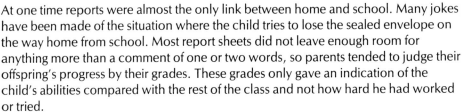

At one time reports were almost the only link between home and school. Many jokes have been made of the situation where the child tries to lose the sealed envelope on the way home from school. Most report sheets did not leave enough room for anything more than a comment of one or two words, so parents tended to judge their offspring's progress by their grades. These grades only gave an indication of the child's abilities compared with the rest of the class and not how hard he had worked or tried.

In order to remedy this situation, reports were devised that had more than one column for grades. The teacher could now give a grade for achievement and effort. But the problem over the comment remained. In secondary schools this form of report has been largely superseded by a report in the form of a booklet in which each subject teacher has a full page to write a comment on the child. Most primary schools have forgone a formal written report and rely on close liaison with parents. In this way any problems can be dealt with as they arise and not at the end of the year. If parents wish to see a school report they are usually referred to their child's record folder or the class teacher writes a letter describing the child's aptitudes and abilities.

As a teacher you may have to write a report at some time, even if it is in the form of the child's record. Here are some hints which I hope may prove helpful.

1 Don't do all your reports in one go. Set aside a period of time e.g. two or three weeks, and do five or six a night.

2 Don't write reports if you are in a really bad mood.

3 Try to make all your comments positive. 'Needs to concentrate more fully on his work' is better than 'Runs wild around the classroom'. The parent might be

tempted to ask why he is allowed to run wild around the classroom whereas if he lacks concentration it's his fault, not yours.

Similarly, although the child may have severe problems while in your class, for example, having been caught stealing, it is not wise to record the child bluntly as being a thief. Children change as they grow older and such a remark can be very damning for a child who erred once. If you feel that the child has a genuine problem, make a remark about lack of trustworthiness and leave the reader to draw their own conclusions in the light of their own knowledge of the child.

4 Most reports/records will ask for comments under headings such as, Language, Maths, Reading, Presentation, Physical Activities, Problems, General Comments, Social and Emotional or Behaviour.

When faced with a blank sheet of paper, it is sometimes helpful to write down ideas under these headings.

5 Always use the same pen for reports so that you can make adjustments or corrections that are not obvious.

6 Don't read the comments of the previous teacher when you write your own. If you do you will find it very difficult to make your comments original. However, do read their comments sometime before you write yours because you do not wish to differ too much, especially if you are finding the child a problem and his last teacher thought he was a little treasure.

It is a well known maxim among teachers that testing only tells you what you knew about the child already — but it makes it official! If used wisely, testing can be a very useful tool for the classroom teacher. Don't test too often — fun though it is — and always bear in mind the limitations of each test. If in doubt, trust your own judgement of the child because this is based on an all-round knowledge of the child as an individual and not on his performance at a specific time on a specific day.

Audio-Visual Aids

The modern teacher has to be familiar with the operation and educational implications of a wide variety of audio-visual aids. Most of these aids are electronic and their use has become widespread only in the last ten years. For the new teacher learning how to operate and maintain these machines can be very off-putting.

However there are two areas of help. Firstly, there is often one person in the school who has bothered to read the instruction booklet and therefore becomes the school 'expert'. This role has great power advantages if all goes well. But you need to be strong to shoulder the guilt when thirty infants don't get their favourite episode of *Words and Pictures*.

Secondly, most of the audio-visual aids found in school are found in the home and many teachers already have a basic knowledge of them, even if the school's models differ from their own.

So what are the advantages of using audio-visual equipment as aids to teaching:

1 It offers a different learning experience for the children. When children are stuck with the same teacher day after day, experiencing the same voice, mannerisms and, in many cases, jokes, no matter how gifted the teacher, a different voice and a different way of presenting the material must be beneficial.

2 The children are learning and, in some cases, interacting with a variety of stimuli, just as we have in the 'real' world. Some parents may still be wary of modern technology. It is important that the children are used to using all the technology schools can provide to give them the confidence that their parents may lack.

3 Audio-visual aids can bring into the classroom experiences that would otherwise be impossible. For example, television can enhance topic work by showing children the insides of factories or life under the sea. Radio can bring the sounds of a symphony orchestra or imaginative noises for dramatic activities.

4 It is important that children are aware of all sources of information. Classrooms tend to rely heavily on the class teacher and books. In modern society there is a shift in emphasis towards technology, rather than the printed word, providing information. Examples of this are those videos showing new kitchen wonder tools that you see in department stores. Children should be aware of this and able to use all sources of information.

Audio-visual aids in School

In too many schools I have used audio-visual aids I would not tolerate in my own home. Televisions with fuzzy pictures, videos with bad tracking and record players with styli with the sensitivity of a pneumatic drill. If we offer children second-rate audio-visual aids then they are going to perceive the information from the aid as being second rate. They will also begin to misbehave because their concentration will wane with the effort of trying to look at/listen to something which is not clear.

So here are some golden rules concerning audio-visual aids in school:

1 All audio-visual aids should be of good quality. Buy the best the school can afford and don't settle for two of a cheaper model — there is a very good reason why they are that cheap.

2 All audio-visual aids should be well-maintained. If a switch doesn't work it should be repaired and not left because it works if it's wriggled about a bit. While you're wriggling so are your class.

3 All audio-visual aids should be kept clean and dust free. Dust damages most electronic apparatus. Keeping something clean shows respect for it. It also makes it more pleasant to handle.

4 All audio-visual aids should be security marked in some way. The best method for this is writing the school's name in large letters in a prominent position. Yes it is defacing the machine and not as aesthetically pleasing as the small UVA lettering but it will be more likely to deter thieves.

5 All cassette recorders, radios, projectors, screens etc. should be easily portable. Buy machines which have sturdy handles and are box-shaped. With school use any extra protruding bits will soon get knocked off.

6 All equipment should be easy to use. The simpler to operate the better. Salespeople will try to convince you that you really need the latest technological wizardry but if it takes ten minutes to set up with the help of the manual will it really ever be used? Are the switches clearly labelled? Classes can be lost while you fast-forward instead of rewind.

7 Have a storage area for audio-visual equipment so that everyone knows where to find it. Insist that it is returned after use. It is not the most educational experience for two pupils to go round every class looking for the brown tape recorder. If there is a central area, make sure that it is secure. A locked store-room is ideal. Another advantage of a central area is that all the fiddly bits — plug, wires, adapters, headphones can be put into containers and labelled.

8 All staff should be able to use all pieces of equipment. To help with this, have the instruction manual or a card with the salient points near to the machine, or stuck to it! Keep the guarantee in a safe place, possibly in the school office.

9 When buying audio-visual aids ask the advice of your Local Education Authority first, especially if they have a county supplies department. If not try the Advisor for Educational Technology. The advantages of dealing with your LEA are threefold. Firstly, they are dealing with hundreds of schools and have experience of how a variety of models have stood up to use in schools. Secondly, they often have a bulk purchase agreement with the manufacturers which means that they are cheaper than high-street shops. Thirdly, if you buy from the Authority then they often have facilities to repair the appliance if it goes wrong.

10 Audio-visual aids should be used regularly in schools, but only where they provide a valuable learning experience for the pupils and not a rest for the teacher.

11 Where possible the children should be taught to carry, operate and care for the school's equipment, just as they would PE or Maths equipment.

12 Copyright should be honoured. I know that schools are very short of money and that you are breaking copyright in a worthwhile cause but besides breaking the law you are depriving an author or a musician of a well-earned income.

13 All audio-visual aids should be set up and ready before the lesson begins. There is nothing worse than a teacher trying to find the right place on a tape or struggling to put in a film strip while the children run riot. Having your audio-visual aids set up is part of your lesson planning and organisation.

14 Safety should be a primary consideration. All wiring should be checked regularly and only approved plugs and adapters should be used. Leads should not be allowed to trail across the classroom floor. Use a circuit breaker if possible. All fuses should be of the correct value.

Care and Use of Some of the Audio-Visual Aids used in Schools

Television

Controls

These are so common I really do not need to go into detail here.

Care

Under no circumstances should the back of the television be removed. Televisions have components that are live even when the set is switched off. So they are not a good place to leave your cup of coffee!

Using the Television

Most schools use the large screen colour television for class viewing of television programmes, either live or on video. Don't forget that you can also use the television as a monitor screen for the computer if you wish to run a program for the whole class.

If a class of children are watching the television at the same time, they need to be seated in front of the screen if possible. To do this they will need to be seated close together which will probably mean sitting on the floor. This will be more comfortable if the floor is carpeted. The television will probably be above their eye line. Although this makes life easier for children at the back, make sure that the children at the front do not get neck-ache! Similarly don't have the volume too loud. A child's hearing is more sensitive than an adult's and if you increase the volume for the children at the back, you may deafen children at the front!

Try not to position the screen opposite a window as the reflections could be distracting. All wiring should be at the back of the set, well out of the way of small fingers.

The television should be kept on a firm surface. Many Local Authorities provide trollies or stands for this purpose. The television will have to be positioned near an aerial socket. Indoor aerials are not usually successful.

In many schools the use of the television has to be timetabled. A copy of the timetable is kept close to the television so there can be no arguments.

When ad-libbing waiting for your programme to start, turn the volume down. It's much less distracting for the children.

Problems

No picture — check that the socket, video and TV have been switched on. Is the aerial in the socket, TV (and video)? Are you using a channel which is pre-tuned? Is the video channel tuned to the video you are currently using?

Black and white picture on a colour television — is the channel pre-tuned correctly? Is the black and white/colour switch found on some videos, switched to colour?

Video Recorder

There are three main types of video recorder, of which only one is commonly found in schools, the VHS system.

Controls

Most teachers will be aware of how to use a video but the following hints may help.

At the back of the machine

▷ **Aerial in:**   This is the lead from the aerial socket in the wall to the video recorder.

▷ **Aerial out:**   This lead goes from the video to the television.

▷ **Record:**   When pressed this will record whatever appears on your television screen when the video is on. Make sure that the video (not the television) is set to the channel you wish to record.

There may be a *black and white/colour switch*. This will give greater clarity to black and white programmes. It should always be left in the colour position or it may confuse the person who has to use the television after you!

Care

▷ Keep free from dust.

▷ Use a head cleaner regularly.

▷ Don't position too close to the television or you may have interference.

▷ Don't move the video recorder (or tapes) from a cold area to a warm room. Moisture may condense on the tape or parts of the machine and to use the recorder in this condition may result in damage.

▷ Rewind tapes after use.

▷ Keep tapes away from the television, video and any magnetic interference. They should also be kept dust free in their boxes and out of direct heat or sunlight.

▷ Never touch the surface of the tape.

▷ Label all the leads so that they cannot be inserted in the wrong sockets or mixed up.

Using the Video Recorder

In most schools there has to be some form of timetabling for using the video recorder. Having chosen which programmes they wish to video, teachers submit their list to a colleague who then works out the best taping and viewing arrangements. It is helpful if the timetable is kept near the television so any prospective users can see if the video is likely to be taping at the time they wish to use it.

The best arrangement is that a whole series of programmes are recorded on one tape but this relies on two feats of memory. Firstly, that the tape is placed in the recorder just before the programme is due to be recorded and secondly, that having begun to watch the series the tape is left at the correct place to record the next programme. This may sound simple enough so why have I never managed it?

Another way of recording is to tape a whole week's programmes on one tape. But this is much easier if you have a video with a weekly repeat facility. The programmes are fairly easy to find so long as everyone rewinds the tape after it has been used and you have the order of recording.

Once used, the video tapes should be clearly labelled with the week or programmes they contain. If your organisation can run to the numbers when each programme begins and finishes your life will be so much easier.

If you wish to keep recordings, remove the tabs at the back of the tape. If these have been removed and you wish to record on the tape, cover them with some masking tape or sellotape.

Radio

In school these are now usually found combined with cassette recorders but I will deal with them separately.

Controls

Most teachers will know how to operate both a radio and a cassetter recorder but here are hints for their use in school.

Most schools broadcasts are on Radio 4 (92.4 – 95.8 FM, 198kHz 1515m LW). It is helpful if you mark the front of the dial somehow with the position of Radio 4.

Use

Radio programmes are probably best taped and then used at your convenience. Those clever little timing switches which plug into a mains socket are invaluable if, like me, you can never remember to tape your radio programmes because you are so involved with your lesson of the moment.

If you are desperate for a missed programme, you can buy them from the BBC. Write to the address on the timetable they send out every term. A cheaper alternative is to ask around your local schools for someone who is taping the same series and ask if they will make you a copy.

Cassette Recorders/Players

When playing back a tape to a class, use the biggest cassette player you can. The distortion from using too small a player with the volume on full will make listening very unpleasant.

Cassette players are usually bulky and heavy. If you send children to collect one, send three children. Two to carry the cassette recorder and one to carry the lead and open doors.

If you wish to keep the recording on a cassette, remove the tab the back. If later you wish to record over the cassette cover the hole left by the tab with a piece of sellotape.

If you wish a group of children to listen to a programme through headphones see if the school has a headphone adapter. This plugs into the headphone socket of a cassette/player and allows up to six children to listen to the same tape through headphones.

Condenser microphones are built into the machine and are very simple to use. However, they are not very selective and have an irritating habit of recording all erroneous noise. When recording a group of children singing or speaking they must be standing an equal distance from the cassette recorder or one voice may dominate the others on the recording.

Clearly label all tapes and their boxes. If you are up to it, keep a record of the number at the beginning and end of the programme. This is incredibly useful if you can manage it.

Record Players

These have been largely superseded by the more compact and portable cassette players. But you may find one in a cupboard somewhere or your school may have invested in a midi hi-fi system which incorporates a record deck.

Make sure that you change the stylus (needle) regularly. Do not touch the stylus with your fingers. If it becomes clogged with dust, try blowing gently or trying to dislodge it gently with the fibres from the record cleaner. Before you play any record, clean it with a proprietary record cleaner. Do not clean the record cleaner with your hand or fingers. Soiled record cleaners should be thrown away. Excess dust can sometimes be blown off. I have actually seen a teacher clean a record with the sleeve of her cardigan! Don't use warped, scratched or worn records. Any records in this condition are not going to be of a suitable quality to play to children so they should be thrown away. This also applies to records that the children and staff may bring in — not the throwing away but the refusing to play on the school record deck! Don't stop a record half-way through a track. If you have heard enough, turn the volume down and stop the record at the end of the track. When not in use keep records in their sleeves. Store records upright away from heat and strong sunlight. Label all leads and, if necessary, match ends and sockets with coloured nail-varnish.

Use

Many children will have some sort of hi-fi system at home. Some of these systems may be of considerably better quality than anything that a school could afford. Therefore, it is important that if you wish to use a record player in school that both records and deck are taken care of properly to provide the best quality sound reproduction possible. It is helpful if the records are catalogued.

Slide/filmstrip and Film Projectors

Moving film projectors have now largely been superseded by videos but may find that larger schools still have one.

Controls

Dark/medium/bright — these are bulb settings. In a light room you may need the brighter bulb setting.
Forward/reverse — this will move the magazine of slides or film forward or backwards.

Care

Some filmstrip projectors have an attachment so that they can be used for slides. To the uninitiated this attachment can look like a shapeless piece of metal. Be careful that it doesn't get thrown away or lost by accident.

Bulbs are expensive. To prolong the life of your bulb, after use run the projector with the bulb off but the fan on.

Clean the lens with a lens cleaning cloth — not a tissue, handkerchief or fingers. Don't touch the surface of the slide or film with fingers.

Use

Film projectors are very easy to load when you know how. Once you have threaded the film through the first few guides, the projector will do the rest automatically. Sometimes there is a diagram of how to do this in the projector box. If not ask a colleague to show you.

When using slides or a filmstrip, ask a child to help you by either holding the excess slides as you change them manually, pressing the forward button to see the next slide or turning the spool to the next frame in the filmstrip. This frees you to give your talk at the front of the class and to point out details you may wish the class to see.

Slides usually go in upside down and back to front. Before loading a whole magazine check one slide first. Children find back to front or upside down pictures incredibly funny. If you are loading slides manually, turn them in their box the correct way round for loading into the projector.

Don't forget to rewind films and filmstrips at the end of the lesson.

Troubleshooting

▷ **No light:** Is the power on and are all leads secure? Is the bulb in the projector properly? Is the bulb broken? Is the bulb switch to either medium or bright?

▷ **Film/magazine sticks:** Is it threaded into the machine correctly? Is one of the slides a different size to the others?

▷ **Fuzzy image:** Is the film/slide loaded correctly? Have you tried focussing the lens? Is the lens clean? Is the screen flat?

Computers

Most schools have at least one computer and they have probably caused more fear and dread than taking the most boisterous of classes. All specific information in this section refers to the BBC Microcomputer (model B) which is by far the most common of the makes found in the Primary school. With a small amount of adaptation the instructions should also work for the Model A and the BBC Master.

Controls

The 'computer' consists of hardware and software. The hardware is the expensive part.

▷ The keyboard (the part usually referred to as the computer).

▷ The monitor/Visual Display Unit (VDU)/television.

▷ A disc drive either floppy 5¼ in. discs or compact 3½ in. discs. The disc drive can be single sided (drive 0) or double sided (drive 0 and drive 2). The drive can also be 40 track, 80 track or both.

▷ A cassette tape recorder.

▷ A printer.

The software are the discs, tapes and programs.

Care

▷ Keep dust free.

▷ Try not to twist the ribbon leads.

▷ Do not touch the surface of the disc.

▷ Do not write on the disc.

▷ Do not turn the computer on or off with the disc in the disc drive.

You cannot harm the computer by typing anything in on the keyboard.

Use

Setting up the computer

▷ Plug in computer, monitor and disc drive.

▷ Turn on monitor (on/off switch is usually found at the back).

▷ Turn on disc drive (on/off switch usually found at the back).

▷ Turn on the computer (on/off switch is on the back).

▷ The screen should now show:

B.B.C Computer 32k

Acorn DFS

BASIC

Insert disc in disc drive (side with exposed area of disc goes in first).

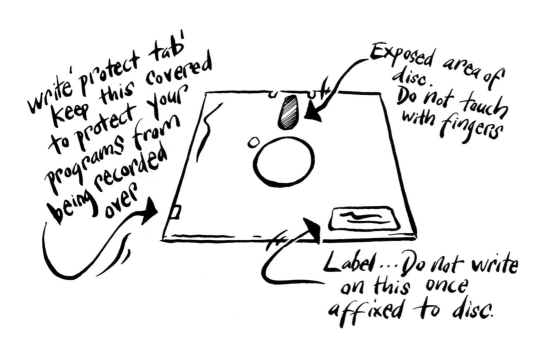

write' protect tab'
keep this covered
to protect your
programs from
being recorded
over

Exposed area of
disc.
Do not touch
with fingers

Label ... Do not write
on this once
affixed to disc.

To Load a Program

Many commercial programs have an auto-start (called a 'boot') which can be activated by holding down a shift key and pressing the break key at the same time. The disc-drive should then start to hum and your program should load.

If you are loading a program from a school disc, type in:

Load 'name of program' and press 'RETURN'

If you are not sure if your program is on that particular disc you will need to look at the disc's catalogue of programs. This is done by typing:

*   and pressing 'RETURN'

If you have a double sided disc drive and you wish to check the catalogue of programs on the other side of the disc, type:

* 2   and press 'RETURN'

To Stop/Escape from a Program

If you wish to stop a program press:

'ESCAPE'

This may not work on some commercial discs and you may have to press:

'BREAK'

If this does not work try pressing:

'CTRL' and 'BREAK'

If this fails you will have to turn off the computer and start again.

If you (or a child) accidently press break and you lose your program, type in:

'old' and press 'RETURN'
and   'run' and press 'RETURN'

Other Useful Keys

▷ 'DELETE' will delete mistakes. Press once for each letter or hold down for longer passages.

▷ 'COPY' use this key to copy anything followed by the shadow cursor.

Computers are happy being left on for long periods of time. This is better than constantly turning them on and off.

When plugging in a disc drive or printer in the sockets under the computer, line up the arrow on the computer with the red line on the side of the ribbon lead. This will make sure you do not plug in the lead the wrong way round.

The capital letters on the keyboard can confuse children if they are not used to capitals.

Check the program you wish to use before you give it to the children. It can be very embarrassing if they ask you for help and you end up getting them all killed by trolls.

Remember that you will need to set the sound fairly high for use in a busy classroom.

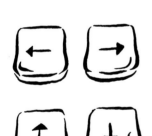

These keys control the cursor (the little white rectangle which tells you where you are).

Formatting and Making Backup Copies of Discs

Before a disc can be used it has to be formatted i.e. introduced to the computer. With your disc drive there should be a formatting disc. A formatting program is already built into the BBC Master.

To format a disc

▷ Put the formatting disc into the disc drive (unnecessary if you have a Master).

▷ Type in:
    *form 40 (for 40 track drives) or
    *form 80 (for 80 track drives)

▷ The computer will then ask you which drive you wish to format.

▷ This will usually be side 0.

▷ The computer will then say:
    'format 40 track drive 0 Go Y/N'

▷ At this point take out the formatting disc and put in the disc you wish to format.

▷ Then press:
    'Y'

There should then be a coloured diagram showing how the formatting is progressing.

▷ When the formatting is complete the computer will tell you that it was successful and ask you if you wish to do another disc. It is easier to do a whole box of new discs at one time. If you have a double-sided disc drive it is easier to do all one side and then the other.

▷ Make at least two backups of discs. One is locked away, one is the backup and the third can be used.

▷ To make a backup of a disc (only if this is permitted under the copyright of the disc) type in:
    *enable
    *backup 0 0 (if you are using a single disc drive) or
    *backup 0 1 (if you are using a double disc drive)

▷ The computer will then say:
    'copying from 0 0
    Go Y/N?'

▷ You type:
    'Y'

The computer will then tell you where to put the source disc and drive disc. Don't forget to press 'RETURN' after every instruction. The source disc is the disc you wish to copy from. The destination disc is the disc you wish to copy to. To prevent an accidental mistake, make sure that your source disc has a 'write protect' tab over the small square cut-out in one side. When the copying is complete the > cursor will appear.

If you are really wary of using the computer, get the children to set it up for you. A few well-trained monitors can save you a lot of heartache as well as face!

Trouble shooting

If anything goes wrong, check the following:

▷ Is the computer set up properly?

▷ Are all leads secure?

▷ Is the disc formatted? Loaded properly?

▷ Type in '*.' to see the catalogue of programs on drive 0. Check to see if the program you wish to use is there.

▷ Try another disc to see if the fault is with the computer or the disc.

▷ If the fault is the disc, make another copy.

▷ If the fault is the computer and you have checked all the above — get help.

▷ If a program 'crashes' in the middle and you have to press 'BREAK', after the screen has cleared try typing in 'OLD'. The program may still be in the computer's memory with the children's work intact.

Epidioscope

This is an old-fashioned but useful machine which you may find in the back of a cupboard. It looks like a large projector with a tray or shelf underneath. The epidioscope is used for projecting items (usually pages from books or pictures) on to a screen.

Care

As for projectors.

Use

As well as being useful for showing the whole class pages from a book or some other special item, the epidioscope is also useful for enlarging diagrams for display purposes. Project the diagram or picture onto your sheet of paper fixed to the wall. You may have to move the machine backwards and forwards until the image is the correct size. When everything is satisfactory draw round the image onto the paper.

Troubleshooting

There is very little that can go wrong with an epidioscope.

Sometimes you may find it difficult to bring a picture into sharp focus. This may be because you are using a picture from near the beginning or end of a thick book so that when it is open under the epidioscope the picture is slanting. Try putting some books underneath so that the book lies flat.

Over-Head Projectors (OHP)

This is a projector where an image from a transparent sheet is projected onto a wall or screen. The transparent sheet can be written on with permanent or wipe-off pens, or some photocopiers will photocopy onto transparent sheets for OHPs. Some OHPs have transparent sheets on a roll.

Use

OHPs are very simple to use and many teachers will use them in preference to a chalkboard. The advantages are that you can prepare your sheets in advance and that you can face your class while writing. The disadvantages of the OHP are that the sheets can be easily smudged and that they can be difficult to focus.

Focussing is achieved by turning the knob on the side of the machine to alter the distance between the lens and the transparent sheet. The lens is tilted to the angle required to project the image on the wall or screen. If you wish the image to be very large it will probably be wedge-shaped and you will lose clarity at the edges. You may have to move the transparent sheet up or down for your audience to see the whole image.

Care

The sheets need to be stored carefully if they are not to become smudged. A storage box for LP records is ideal.

Troubleshooting

You may find difficulty in focussing the OHP to achieve the image size that you require. Try moving the machine the distance needed from the wall/screen until the image is the size you want and then try to focus it by adjusting the lens distance.

You may have to refocus the machine for every sheet. If the sheet is not flat you may not be able to have it all in focus.

Heat Copiers

These have now largely fallen out of favour owing to the availability of photocopiers. However, they do have one very useful aspect. They are able to make a banda master of something you wish to copy.

Photocopiers

Many schools are now able to afford to rent a small, desk top photocopier and then wonder how they ever lived without it!

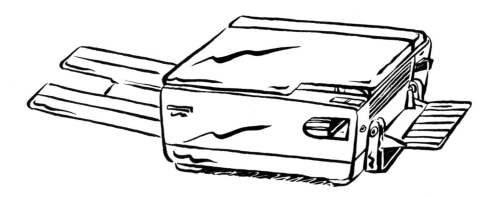

Depending on the sophistication of the photocopier there may also be controls for reducing and enlarging and for making colour copies.

Care

Photocopiers need little routine maintenance that can be performed by the school. On some models the toner can be changed by the school as it is a complete unit, but for most makes of machine the manufacturers will need to deal with any problems.

Use

Photocopiers are very easy to use. There are guidelines printed around the edge of most machines so that you put your original in the correct place. The only other thing to remember is that the side you wish to copy goes face down and to make a note of which way round the copies come out if you wish to copy on both sides!

Some photocopiers will copy onto acetate sheets so that overhead transparencies are possible.

Some schools redeem some of their rental money by offering a photocopying facility to friends of the school at a reduced rate.

Controls

▷ **On/off**

▷ **Ready Light/Symbol:**   This will appear/go out when the machine has been on for enough time to be warmed up and ready for use.

▷ **Lighter/Darker:**   This controls how light or dark the final copies will be. Most of the time it will remain in the middle but when copying from coloured paper you may need to adjust it to achieve the maximum detail on the copy.

▷ **Number of copies:**   On most machines you can pre-set the number of copies you need. This is useful if you wish to do a large number of copies because it means you can go away and do something else while the machine is copying.

▷ **Toner Low:**   A symbol will light when the photocopier needs more toner.

▷ **Paper Low:** A symbol will light when the machine needs more paper in the paper feed.

Troubleshooting

▷ **Copies too dark:** Move lighten/darken control towards lighten.

▷ **Copies too light:** Move lighten/darken controls towards darken.

▷ **Not all of your original has copied:** Is the original in the correct place for the size of paper you are using? Has anyone left the reduce/enlarge controls on the wrong size for the copies you want?

▷ **Paper jams:** Before consulting the manual to find out how to take the machine to pieces try removing as much of the jammed paper as you can reach. Turn the machine off and then back on again. Sometimes it will then clear itself.

Blackboard/Chalkboard/Whiteboard

The traditional symbol of the teaching profession and an audio-visual aid to which most teachers will have access.

If you are fortunate to have a chalkboard in good condition try to keep it that way. Don't wash it. Clean it with a soft duster or board-rubber which should be cleaned regularly. (Outside, preferably. This is a good, practical exercise to help gauge in which direction the wind is blowing.) A chalkboard with a very bad surface can be repainted with special paint, available from the local Authority Supplies or specialist art/craft shops. However, the paint will not give such a smooth surface as proper reconditioning of the chalkboard, but it does mean you can paint a chalkboard wherever you would like one.

Some teachers dealing with difficult children have an area of wall painted as a chalkboard just for them. The children are free to go and write or draw anything they like on their chalkboard. The only rule is that they must always wipe it off afterwards. The teachers have found that this relieves some of the pent-up frustrations and emotions of these children which is usually manifested in anti-social or anti-authority aggression. These chalkboard areas are usually out of the way so that the child is as private as he can be when he uses the chalkboard and it is not the first thing that visitors see when they enter the classroom!

When using a chalkboard:

Break a new piece of chalk in half before you use it — or it will break before you finish your first word and ping across the room, to your embarrassment and the glee of the children.

When writing on the chalkboard, don't write as if you are using a pen i.e. with your fingers. Move your whole arm to form the shapes. This is very tiring, especially if you have to reach up or down. (Some teachers use writing on a chalkboard to cure children of the 'crab' posture when handwriting).

Always write on the chalkboard in the style in which you wish the children to write.

Try underlining the date before you write it — it will look neater.

White shows up best on a dark coloured chalkboard. I think yellow is second best. If you want to give instructions to children on the chalkboard followed by a piece of work to copy, try training the children to read yellow words (instructions) and only copy white words (work).

Useful pieces of equipment are a chalkboard ruler, a chalkboard setsquare and a chalkboard compass. The compass is especially useful because you can use it to draw large circles for display etc.

Even the 'anti-dustless' chalk we now use creates a large amount of dust so asthmatics should be placed away from the chalkboard, while children with sight problems should be placed directly in front of it.

School Trips and Visits

At some time you may wish to take children out of school, either for an excursion into your locality; to another school for a sports or music event; for a day visit or for a longer residential visit. Each of these visits poses their own particular problems.

To help you with the wealth of legal regulations about taking children out of school, your Education Authority probably has a file listing its own regulations. Your Headteacher should have it buried somewhere in his office. These are guidelines which you will have to follow in order to be covered legally and by the County insurance policies. These regulations vary from County to County so the information I give here is really only for general guidance.

There are many reasons for taking children out of the classroom environment and all of them have sound educational principles. But basically we take children out of the classroom on two types of visit. Firstly to supplement work that is done in the classroom and secondly as a recreational visit where the educational value is social and in gaining experiences that could not be achieved by any other means. The first type of visit is usually arranged in school time e.g. a visit to:

a museum
an historical monument
a place of interest
a field studies centre

The second type of visit is usually arranged out of school time e.g. a visit to:

a theatre
a concert
a skiing holiday

Under the terms of the *1988 Education Act* parents are not required to pay for any school visit which is deemed 'essential', 'compulsory' or 'forming part of the school curriculum'. Voluntary contributions may be requested but it must be made clear to parents that payments are not compulsory and no child can be excluded from a school visit because his parents have declined to pay their voluntary contribution.

How to Organise a School Visit

1 Choose where you wish to go. This may be linked to work you are doing/will be doing in the classroom or may be the opportunity to take advantage of a special experience you feel may benefit the children.

2 Ask permission to go from your Headteacher, Head of Year or other senior staff. The school governors are informed of all school visits in the termly headteacher's report. If you wish to take the children abroad or on a residential visit you may need the permission of your governors and your Local Education Authority.

3 Ask your colleagues to see if anyone would like to come with you. Two classes on a visit can be cheaper than one.

4 Find out entrances fees, opening times etc. and book a provisional date.

5 Work out the transport costs. Methods of transporting children are:

▷ **Parents' cars:**   This is the cheapest method, but only really suitable for small groups such as school teams in the local area. Some Local Education Authorities insist that parents carrying children in cars must have suitable insurance.

▷ **Coach:**   This is the most popular method of transporting children. It is convenient. The children are transported from door to door and you have shelter for lunch if it rains. The children can also leave behind on the coach any bulky belongings that are not needed.

▷ **Train:**   This is reasonably priced and can be useful if you have a mainline station within walking distance of the school. Rail travel does provide an extra experience for the children, many of whom will not have travelled by rail before. You will need more supervisory adults than travelling by coach. It is less flexible and you will have to carry everything around with you all day.

6 Work out the cost of the visit. Your accounts must be available for inspection by parents so make sure you have your maths right!

7 Confirm the booking and the transportation in writing. Make sure that arrival and departure times are clear.

8 Send out a letter to parents explaining the purpose of the visit, in good time.

A sample letter:

Anytown Primary School,
School Lane,
Anytown,
Countyshire,
AB1 2CD

Dear Parents,

In connection with their work on Castles, we have arranged for Classes 3 and 4 to visit the Tower of London on Friday 20th May. The coach will leave at 9.15 a.m. and we expect to be returning to school at about 5.30 p.m. If you wish your child to be dropped off the coach before arrival back at school, would you please indicate at which stop on the form below.

Children will need a packed lunch (no glass bottles please) and we would appreciate school uniform with suitable walking shoes. There is a gift shop at the Tower so your child may like to take a small amount of pocket money, for example £2. Cameras may be taken at the owner's risk.

The cost of the visit is £2 for the coach and £1 entrance fee. We would welcome any voluntary contributions by parents to help cover costs.

If you wish your child to go on the visit please sign the form below.

Yours sincerely,

I. Teachem

Class Teacher

— —

I give permission for my child ....Class ......
to go on the school visit to the Tower of London

I would like my child to leave the coach at:

* The Clock Tower
* The War Memorial
* The High Street
* The Coach and Horses
* Anytown School

* Please delete as applicable.

9 Make arrangements for children not going on the visit.

10 See dining staff about cancelling dinners for that day and arranging a packed lunch for the free school dinner children.

11 Ask for helpers. To take children out of school there has to be a greater ratio of adults to children than the usual 1:30. Your Local Education Regulations should tell you how many adults you will need for your age of children. But for general

guidance you will need 1 adult to ten infants and 1 adult to fifteen juniors. In reality you may wish to take more adults (I would) and arrange your class in groups of 5–7 with an adult in charge of each group. It is customary to ask first those helpers who regularly come into the school, for example to hear children read. Make sure you have a reserve should a helper be unable to come on the day.

On The Day

1 Make sure you are at school early to deal with any last minute problems.

2 Wear something bright and easily recognisable so that the children can see you from a distance.

3 If your school has a uniform, ask the children to wear it. It makes your job much easier in trying to keep track of them. For some visits school uniform will obviously be impractical. Younger children may need to be labelled with their name and school.

4 Write the names of the group leaders and their groups on the chalkboard. Give a list of the children in their groups to each helper. Some children like to go with their mothers. Some mothers do not want to be with their children. You will have to make discreet enquiries if you have a mother coming along as a helper. You keep all potential troublemakers in your group.

5 Collect together everything that you are going to need:

  ▷ List of children going and their groups

  ▷ List of which children are leaving the coach before reaching school

  ▷ Paperwork for visit — tickets, plans etc

  ▷ Bin liners — for rubbish and to sit on

  ▷ First Aid Kit (or two for a large party)

  ▷ Sick bags (Please, not polythene bags, for obvious reasons)

  ▷ Money

  ▷ Travelsickness tablets and any other medicines any child may need to take

  ▷ Camera

  ▷ Umbrella, unless sunshine guaranteed

  ▷ Tissues/paper towels

  ▷ Spare plastic bag for the drink that always leaks

6 Before leaving school insist that all children have a toilet visit.

7 On a train the children will have to sit with their group leader. On a coach they can fill up in pairs from the front.

8 The rules on a coach will depend on the individual teachers concerned but generally it is wise not to allow the children to kneel up on the seats; stand; change seats; eat (unless travel sick); shout or sing — unless you have particularly strong nerves or a guitar and boundless energy.

9 If a child feels travel sick, bring him to the front of the coach, provide plenty of fresh air and a boiled sweet if possible. Talk to him to take his mind off the nausea. When he has his colour back, you know that the danger is over. Don't let the other children see him vomit or you will have many more cases of travelsickness on your hands.

10 When you arrive, arrange a time and place to meet up for lunch/to go home.

11 When supervising a crocodile of children, make sure you have two trusted children at the front. These children need to be taught to walk slowly and to look back to see that the rest of the class is keeping up. It is best if the teacher is near the back of the line so that you can keep an eye on most of the class. If there is a road to cross stop the children at the kerb. The teacher goes out and stops the traffic. The children cross and wait for her at a pre-arranged place at the other side. This means that the front of the line does not charge off into the wide blue yonder while you are saving the back from a large articulated lorry.

12 Allow the children time to visit the shop at the end of the visit.

13 Allow time for a toilet stop before you leave.

14 Count the children or take a register before you finally leave. If you do lose a child, leave one teacher behind to deal with the problem and make sure that she has all the telephone numbers she is likely to need and enough money to get home.

15 When the children leave the coach at any stop other than the school, make sure that you have their parent's permission and that a parent is there to meet them. If they live in a house very close to the stop, wait and watch to see that the child enters the home safely. There will be always one child who isn't collected on time so warn your own family not to expect you for at least an hour after the official arrival time and if the trip is in the winter, have a torch with you.

A last few helpful hints. Never tell children that 'there's only another half an hour to go before we get there' or 'we're nearly there now'. Children have no concept of time and will plague you with 'Are we nearly there now?' after the first ten minutes on the coach. Always tell them that there is a long journey still to go and they will leave you alone.

Losing children is every teacher's nightmare and despite the best of precautions it is very easily done. To help children who may become lost, show them an easily recognisable meeting place. Don't just say 'We'll meet back at the coach'. They will have no idea where the coach is unless you give them a landmark close by such as a church steeple or advertisement board. It is wiser to tell children who have become separated by accident to stay where they are so that you can retrace your steps and find them. This is where a school uniform is very useful.

Residential Visits

The organisation for these is similar to a day visit except that you will have to know if any of the children have any special requirements, e.g. for food or health.

If you are travelling abroad, apply for your group passport in good time. This can be very complicated if one of the children was born abroad.

You may like to give children (and parents) a handbook for the visit which should give them all the information they require to prepare for the visit.

The handbook could include:

▷ A list of children and adults going on the visit

▷ A list of items and clothing children will need to take with them. This list will obviously vary according to the type of visit you are going on but here is a list for a four day visit of Upper Juniors to Belgium which may offer some suggestions:

Each child will need:

1 A sleeping bag which should not be packed in the case as all sleeping bags will be loaded together on to the coach. It would help if the sleeping bag could be packed in a protective plastic bag with identification label attached.

2 A small light bag (a nylon rucksack type would be ideal).

In this you should take:

▷ Packed lunch and drink. The drink should be in a plastic re-usable container which may be used during the course of the trip.

▷ A light, waterproof coat, e.g. a cagoule type

▷ A game and/or book to pass time on the journey

▷ Camera and binoculars if taken

3 The main case to contain:

▷ tee-shirts/shirts for four days plus one spare

▷ underwear for same period

▷ socks for same period

▷ 2 towels

▷ washing gear and brush/comb etc.

▷ pyjamas/nightdress

▷ outdoor and indoor shoes

▷ warm jumpers or sweatshirts

▷ trousers/skirts for smart wear and play

▷ pillow case

▷ swimming costume (which we may need)

▷ small pocket torch

▷ plastic bag for dirty clothing

▷ toilet paper/tissues

4 Valuables: You may take a camera or binoculars with you but they must be your responsibility. It is advisable to buy film in this country. Please keep jewellery to a minimum.

5 Pocket Money: The amount will depend on you but it is easier if the money is entrusted to a member of staff for safe keeping. As well as avoiding theft this also stops the children spending all their money at the first gift shop.

▷ Please make sure that all items are clearly labelled with their owner's name.

▷ An address and emergency telephone number

▷ A timetable and itinerary

▷ Telephone chain

e.g.

The teacher in charge of the party telephones the first parent in the chain who then telephones the second parent and so on. This can be used to tell parents of the safe arrival of the children and, if the first parent is telephoned about an hour's travelling time away from school, when the party are likely to be arriving back at school. The chain can also be used during the visit for an emergency.

▷ An alternative method of letting parents know of the safe arrival of their offspring is that each child posts a pre-written postcard to their parents on the evening of their arrival.

▷ It is also helpful to warn children (and parents) if there is to be an end of visit party which may need fancy dress.

Preparing for the visit

To gain the maximum benefit from a school visit there needs to be some preparation or follow-up activity connected with it. The visit itself may be the starting point or climax to a class's work.

The visit as a starting point

1 Make sure the children know that they are going to have to do some work on the subject matter of the visit.

2 Make sure that you point out the items of interest concerning the work they are going to do later.

3 Try to stimulate their interest in the subject.

4 Use the visit to acquire any materials which may be useful later back in the classroom.

The visit as a climax

1 Make sure the children have covered the subject matter in order to gain the maximum benefit from the visit.

2 Enjoy the children's pleasure as they discover the originals of things they may have only seen in books.

3 Point out to children important links between the subject of the visit and their classwork.

Worksheets

These pose a problem. If the children have a worksheet to fill out it does direct their attention to the things that you may wish them to find out but conversely, having endless worksheets to do can spoil the fun of a visit and narrow the children's experience to answer-hunting.

A compromise could be a guided tour where the adult group leader takes her group around the visit and they are asked to think about what they are seeing, by judiciously worded questions. For this to work all group leaders must be aware of the work done in the classroom and know what they must draw the children's attention to.

If you wish to use the pre-prepared worksheets of the place you are going to visit, it is wiser to send for a copy beforehand to see their suitability for your children. You may have to adapt them.

If the children are to use worksheets they will need a pencil, rubber and a board to rest on. A cheap board can be made from the front and back covers of old ring-binders. The children will also need a bulldog clip. You may like to tie the children's pencil to this. However, these boards can be a nuisance to carry and impossible if it is raining.

Seasonal Activities

In primary education teachers tend to take advantage of the seasonal celebrations to supplement their classwork. Children have very little awareness of time, and work on the seasons helps with this concept. Work on celebrations helps to broaden their awareness of our traditions and those of other religious and ethnic groups.

The Main Festivals

Makar Sankranti/Lohri (Hindu) around January 12th

Winter solstice. A time for making peace with the neighbours.

Chinese New Year (Cultural festival) January/February

This begins with the first new moon between January 21st and February 19th

Easter (Christian) March/April

A festival commemorating Christ's resurrection.

Baisakhi (Sikh) April 13th or 14th

Sikh New Year

Pesach or Passover (Jewish) April

This festival remembers the deliverance of the Jews from slavery in Egypt.

The Feast of Ridvan (Baha'i) April 21st – May 2nd

A festival to commemorate the declaration of Baha'u'llah's mission.

Wesak (Buddhist) late May/early June

A festival celebrating the birth, death and enlightenment of Buddha.

Birthday of Haile Selassie 1 (Rastafarian) July 23rd

One of the holiest days of the Rastafarian year.

Yom Kippor (Jewish) October

The Day of Atonement is the most important day in the Jewish calendar.

Divali (Hindu) October/November

A festival of lights. The Hindu New Year begins at the end of Divali.

Christmas (Christian) December 25th

A festival celebrating the birth of Christ.

Hanukkah (Jewish) December

A festival of lights remembering the dispersal of the Jews.

Ramadan (Muslim) different times of the year

A month of fasting. Abstinence from food and drink from dawn to sunset for purification of body and soul.

Eid ul-Fitr (Muslim)

Feast day at the end of the period of fasting. (Ramadan)

If you teach in a school with children from different faiths try to be aware of their festivals and celebrations as the year progresses. Often children can be very shy and embarrassed at the rites they have to follow because of their religious faith. If you can, try to encourage the child to share his festival with the rest of the class. If the other children are aware of the symbolism behind the child's dress, food or behaviour, they are more likely to be interested and understanding. Some parents may even come and talk to your class.

Unless you have children from different faiths in your class, it is probably a better idea to introduce the various festivals as part of a theme. Ideas for this might include: light, food, dress, holy people, buildings, signs and symbols etc.

Titles of same useful publications can be found in *Appendices*.

Beginning the School Year

Check that you have everything ready in your classroom. (see Chapter on *Classroom Organisation* for list of stock etc.) The beginning of the year is when you lay down the foundations of your discipline (see Chapter of *Discipline, Punishments and Rewards*). The first few days' lessons are probably the hardest of the whole year to teach because your children have no on-going pieces of work and you are not certain of their ability.

Try to have work that they can do which needs little input from you. The usual standbys are work about themselves or the holiday they have just had. Don't forget to tell the children when their PE/swimming lessons take place so that they can bring in their kit.

Six weeks is a long time in the life of a child. Don't judge them on their first week's work. Any testing is best left until the second or third week of term when they have settled back into the school routine.

One last word of warning about the beginning of the year. Even experienced teachers are surprised at how little their new class can do when they first get them. There is a whole year's difference between the third years who have just left you and the new third years in front of you.

Autumn

Now is a good time to begin any work on the seasons as summer has just gone and the other three will pass before your present class leave you. The class could look at a tree, or a patch of ground or the school grounds generally to study the difference the seasons make to our environment. Weather is another good year-round topic.

Another year-long activity you may wish to begin is to weigh and measure the children regularly. This will teach them about histograms (if you wish to record it that way) but it will also give you an indication of any weight or growth problems.

Hallowe'en (31st October)

Many schools frown upon work done about Hallowe'en, but there is no doubt that children love it and that ideas for Hallowe'en are endless.

Harvest Festival

This usually comes too soon after the beginning of the year when you are just getting used to your class. Most schools have some form of Harvest Festival service, with

contributions from each class. Some schools ask for harvest gifts from the children and these are given away to some needy cause. Here are some of the ways of dealing with Harvest:

1 The history of the Harvest Festival service itself. (There is no room to print it here but it is very interesting.)

2 Take a theme such as: giving, sharing, thankfulness, water, bread, food.

3 Different types of harvests.

Harvest may be one of the few times of year that your children go to church. Children who do not go to church regularly with their families may be at a loss as to how to behave. A few words of warning (or even some RE lessons about the church building) can save you a lot of embarrassment and the church from getting muddy kneelers.

It is useful to have a rehearsal in the church as the acoustics are usually poorer than the average school hall. Also the children will have to know where to sit. Remember they will have to sit in reverse order so that they are correctly positioned as they leave the pew. If they are capable, have them move into position during the last verse of the preceding hymn. Make it clear who is going to lead back to the pew or else you will have a free-for-all as they try to sit in their original positions. Children can be very territorial.

It can be very difficult to deal with trouble makers if they are at the end of the pew in front. Give plenty of threats and sit any potential trouble makers next to you. Give them the responsibility of looking after your hymn book or something. Don't hiss at children to be quiet in a church. The sound carries embarrassingly!

Many schools have the tradition of giving harvest gifts to needy members of the local community. These may be old folk or a local children's home etc. The children are asked to provide the names and addresses of people to whom they would like to give a harvest gift and they are usually responsible for delivering it. The harvest gifts that the children bring are usually shared between the number of names you have been given.

This activity is wonderful for introducing division and equality — do two carrots equal one cabbage? etc.

You will also need something to put the harvest gifts in and a 'with compliments' slip to show who the gift is from. A plastic carrier bag is cheap and easily obtainable but not very special. Try approaching a local shoe shop for some spare shoe boxes. If they have a few weeks warning they are usually quite happy to keep thirty or so shoe boxes for you which would otherwise be destroyed.

Some parents will make up a box of harvest gifts especially for the person who is to receive the gift. If you wish to encourage this then you must ask parents to make it clear that they have done this. If you wish to share all gifts then you must make this plain to parents who may like to add their own special ideas later.

Fireworks/Bonfire Night (November 5th)

This comes too quickly after Hallowe'en for most teachers. (Why couldn't something exciting have happened in the Spring Term?) For older children there is an excellent television programme about the Gunpowder Plot in the BBC series *Now and Then*. As for Hallowe'en, ideas for creative work etc. are legion.

Christmas

Productions

Many schools put on a formal production with a Christmas theme at the end of the Autumn Term. Ideally, the Christmas production should be planned before the end of the previous summer term so that everyone has a chance to get the scripts, music etc. sorted out in good time. If it is left until half term then pressures of time tend to be more acute and frayed nerves and tempers result.

1   A dramatised version of the biblical story, perhaps with relevant carols breaking up the action. (Very sweet with young children but a bit old hat for top juniors, Joseph is usually very difficult to cast in a class of eleven year olds.)

2   A new slant of the biblical story, for example, set in modern times or space travellers returning to biblical times. (This usually works well and keeps everyone happy.)

3   An improvised play of a Christmassy story e.g. *Papa Panov, A Christmas Carol, Baboushka.* (Good if you've a self confident class used to role play activities.)

4   A published play. This requires much more work from everyone and the children have to be really keen to learn pages of lines. You also have to watch royalty fees and write in good time to get permission to perform the play. A good compromise is to write one yourself because then you can fit parts and language to the children but this is really a labour of love and often not feasible at this time of year.

Now you have decided what you are doing it is a good idea to have someone in overall charge with everyone else contributing help in a specific area; e.g. Mrs X is in charge of the production, Miss Y will do all music and songs, Mr Z will do all scenery and props. Putting on a production is a big strain on teachers at the end of an exhausting term and having separate areas of responsibility does save the children being given conflicting instructions by teachers who visualise the play in different ways. Of course this will only work if Mrs X has given Miss Y and Mr Z clear instructions as to what she wants, and has given them in plenty of time.

You can have someone in charge of costumes or even in charge of some helpful parents who are prepared to give up time to make all the costumes, but it is better not to give any choice. If they want to be in the play then they have to come up with a costume. However in certain circumstances this will have to be tempered with an understanding of the child's background. I have found it useful to ask the children to bring their costume to the dress rehearsal in a named carrier-bag or on a named coat hanger which they then leave ready for the performance. This way no-one argues over belts or tea-towels and no-one forgets their costume. It is best if infants arrive wearing their costumes (although I have had one child turning up dressed as a shepherd to a pantomime performance of Cinderella. The Carol Service tableaux was the next day!)

Children do not like to practise and generally have no sense of quality. They know their parents are going to think they're wonderful and they do not really care if the Chairman of Governors is sitting in the middle of the front row and you have just applied for a new post. There are two ways to rehearse. Little and often over the whole term (some schools even start before the summer holidays) or solidly for two weeks before the night. Both of these have obvious advantages but one must beware of beginning the first and doing the second anyway! It helps the children if they have a specific time in which to learn their words, half term is ideal. It doesn't really help to yell at them when rehearsing although it does relieve a lot of your own pent-up frustration, I know. Try to show them what you want them to do and over-dramatise it, then if the child meets you half way you have probably got the acting you wanted.

Plays require an awful lot of work and it is a shame to have it all finished within one evening. Showing the play (or plays) over two evenings has many advantages. It usually means that most parents will be able to come on one or the other nights (often Mum comes on one night while Dad babysits and on the second night they change places.) It can be a good idea to ask parents beforehand for numbers of seats required and which is their preferred night. However, do make sure that the children know that *they* have to be there on both nights.

Try to include all children in productions and often children who do not wish to be on stage are trustworthy and reliable musicians, props managers and scene shifters. A good way to include everyone (especially in the smaller school) is to have some songs. It is much better if the children learn the words of the songs and stand with their hands in front of them or by their sides. A fidgeting choir can ruin a performance. Stress that the choir are also on show and try to dress them in a suitable 'costume' as well, even if it is strict school uniform.

The Carol Service

The service of Nine Lessons and Carols is always a good standby but often biblical language is very difficult for the children to understand and most adults have heard it umpteen times before anyway. A variation is to use Christmassy readings of poems or extracts or even (and I'm a great believer in this) the children's own work.

Now might be a good time to mention children reading. Most children read too quickly and too softly. Even if you pick the most raucous voice in the playground, when it comes to reading in public you will be surprised as to how genteel they will be. Obviously the child must have the words in good time to practise. Don't let the child write out the words. You do it or type it (although typing is often too small. The Jumbo daisy wheel is ideal for this sort of thing). Make the child practise in a large area, the empty hall or across the playground. The classroom is too small. If necessary do not have the child at the front of the audience, one third of the way forward can help matters considerably, especially in a church. Personally, I dislike seeing children reading from well-thumbed pieces of paper. I have found it useful to mount their work on card and stick a suitable picture on the front. If you have several readers you can even have large letters spelling out a word (but do make sure they know which order to stand in, it's very easy for your readers to become reversed leaving their seats from the wrong end).

For organising the children in a Church much of what I have said in *Harvest* will apply. Although we might be bored with the 'traditional' carols they are still new to the children, and the parents will only be able to join in with these. It is nice to have the children singing some less usual carols and it may even broaden their parents' repertoire!

Christmas Dinner

Every school has its own traditions for Christmas Dinner but if you feel that it's time for a change here some ideas.

1 Children have Christmas dinner served to them by staff dinner ladies or older children (preferably dressed up). Adult Christmas dinner could then be after school.

2 Children dress up or wear special hats for Christmas dinner. The same dress/hat could be used for their parties.

3 Carols sung by the choir/volunteers/anyone/on a record help make the atmosphere more festive.

4 Simple table decorations and place-names can be made as shown:

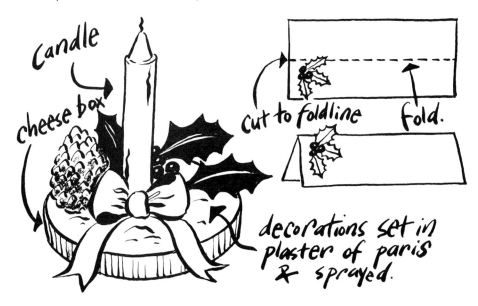

Candle

cheese box

cut to foldline   fold.

decorations set in plaster of paris & sprayed.

5 Governors could be invited to the adult Christmas lunch so they can be suitably impressed with your Christmas displays.

6 Children with special diets or with a packed lunch should be with the other children for this one lunch-time.

7 The lunch-time is usually very long so have a short straw competition as to who goes on duty.

8 A suitable video rounds off the afternoon nicely.

Christmas Parties

These are usually held in class or year groups. The children usually have some firm ideas as to how they would like their party organised (and they have been to more of such parties than the average teacher). Ask them to write out what happened last year and their favourite games. This should give you a structure to work on if you have no experience of children's parties.

Despite your misgivings the time will pass very quickly so here are some suggestions to save your sanity (if not your eardrums!).

Games

There are very many children's games so here is a list of some of the most popular.

Musical Statues

Children dance to the music. When music stops they have to stand still. Anyone moving is out.

▷ **Variations:** Children can adopt a pose e.g. jockey, ballet dancer when music stops.

Children can pass a hat round a circle. Child with hat on head when music stops is out.

Musical Chairs

Put a row of chairs (with large numbers have them facing alternate directions) in the middle of the room; one less than the number of children. Children walk round the chairs. When music stops they must sit down on a chair. Child without a chair to sit on is out. Take away another chair (or two for speed) and start again.

▷ **Variations:** Two children to a chair. One child sitting on another's lap.

Pin the Tail on the Donkey

Have a large drawing of a donkey without a tail. Pin it at child's height to a wall. Make a 'tail' with a pin in the top. Blindfolded child has to pin the tail on the correct part of the donkey. Child nearest to correct position wins.

▷ **Variations:** Tail on any other animal. Beard on Santa Claus.

Team Games

Children have to pass object down the line until it reaches the person at the back. This person then runs with the object to the front and begins to pass it back again. Game ends when first person is at the front of the line again.

▷ **Variations:** Balloons between knees, matchboxes on the ends of noses, oranges under chins, pingpong balls in spoons etc.

Eating the Bar of Chocolate

Children are in teams. They sit in a circle around a plate with a bar of chocolate (which has come from the fridge, if you want to be really mean) a knife and fork, a hat and a pair of gloves (or mittens). The children throw a dice in turn. When a child throws a six, he dons the hat and gloves and tries to eat the chocolate with the knife and fork. He continues to do this until another child throws a six. The team who eat their bar of chocolate first wins. But by this time no-one really cares as the game usually degenerates into chaos, especially if there are several sixes in quick succession.

Pass the Parcel

A perennial favourite. A small prize is wrapped up in layers of paper. The children sit in a ring and pass the parcel until the music stops. The child holding the parcel at that time unwraps one layer. The child who unwraps the last layer wins the prize.

▷ **Variations:** The children can be encouraged to pass the parcel on if there are forfeits between each layer. These can be suited to the age of the children but some ideas are:

▷ say the alphabet (backwards)

▷ make Susie laugh without touching her

▷ sing a nursery rhyme/Christmas carol/hymn

▷ tell a joke

▷ dance a hornpipe

▷ impersonate the Prime Minister/Donald Duck/a teacher

Word Games

A word is written out with the letters mixed up onto a sheet of paper. These words are pinned up around the room. The children have to unscramble the words within a certain amount of time. Child with the most words is the winner. This can also be played as a team game.

Puzzles

Mount several pictures onto coloured card (a different colour for each picture). Cut the pictures up into the same number of pieces and hide these pieces around the room. The teams are given a colour and have to find all the pieces of card in their colour and jig-saw the picture back together. The first team with a complete picture wins.

Winter

Activities for winter will concentrate on

▷ snow and ice

▷ time

▷ diaries

▷ new beginnings

Be warned, many teachers cover these topics in the spring term so order your resources very early.

St. Valentine's Day (February 14th)

This is hard to ignore because of the commercial hype, but making cards can take up an art lesson and the story of St. Valentine or a look at what love means is a good assembly.

Spring/Easter

Common themes are

▷ eggs

▷ tadpoles

▷ seeds

▷ growth

Hatching Eggs

You can usually get some fertilised eggs from a local hatchery. You will need to borrow an incubator from your local secondary school or your science inspector/advisor. The eggs have to be kept at a certain humidity and temperature and the chicks, when they hatch, will not be cute and fluffy. The instruction leaflet with the incubator will tell you what to do but as a general rule, leave the newly hatched chicks in the incubator for another twenty-four hours before transferring them to their run. Do not try to help the chicks to hatch. They are still attached to the inside of their shell and your assistance can be fatal.

When the chicks are ready they can be put into a run. This needs to be kept in a place where the temperature is constantly warm. So your classroom is ideal. An enclosure can be made with tables propped up against each other to form a rough rectangle. The chicks will also need a box to go into at night. Suspend a mop head from the top of the box as a substitute mother hen for the chicks to huddle under. This was fondly known as 'Mummy mop-head' in my school.

Chicken food can be bought at any good animal or pet suppliers and they will eat a lot. They will also need water. The chicks are cute and fluffy for only a few days. After that they become more straggly and begin to grow their adult feathers. At this point the children may be chary of picking them up as they can be rather fierce. Make sure they do not pick on one of their number as chicks have been known to be pecked to death.

When you have finished your project you may wish to give the chicks away or to keep them permanently in the school.

Tadpoles

The children will know where to get frog spawn. You may end up with toad spawn (in strings rather than clumps) but it really doesn't matter. You will need some form of tank in which to keep the tadpoles. An infant water-play tray is ideal. Encourage the children to bring in some pond water and weed so that your aquarium offers the same conditions as the pond. Line the bottom with stones and have some stones breaking the surface of the water for your froglets to sit on. If you are not given enough pond water, do not put the tadpoles straight into tap water. Fill your tank with tap water and leave it for as long as possible before putting in the spawn and anything else you have been given from the pond. Check carefully to see that you have not been given some dragonfly larva as they are voracious carnivores and will eat everything that moves.

For the first few weeks the tadpoles will need very little looking after and the children will begin to become bored with looking at them. Nil desperandum, keep going. It may be that a cold spell has slowed up their development. About the time they grow their back legs they will become carnivorous and will need feeding or else they will eat each other (they may do this anyway). Pieces of meat or cat food are suitable. Suspend the food in the water with a piece of cotton so that you can remove it after 24 hours or else it will turn the water rancid and very, very smelly.

When your little froglets are about 15mm long it will be time to find them a new home. This could be in a school pond or ask the children to take them to local ponds. If you put them into your school pond it will be three years before they will breed in it and you will have your own supply of frog spawn.

Pancake Day/Shrove Tuesday

There is a wealth of work you can do about this. Children love making and tossing pancakes. If you want the children to eat the pancakes they toss, make sure they toss the pancake over a clean area such as a table or a plastic tablecloth.

A very useful poem for pancake day is:

Pancakes

> Mix a pancake,
> Stir a pancake,
>   Pop it in the pan;
> Fry the pancake,
> Toss the pancake, –
>   Catch it if you can.

Christina Rossetti

Games Rallies and Matches

You may have to organise a team for a rally or match. Once you have chosen your children here are some things to remember.

1 Send out letters to parents asking permission for the child to attend the match/rally. Many Local Authorities have standard letters but if you have to write your own then the following letter may be useful as a guide.

```
Dear Parents,

Your child has been chosen to play in the school football/
netball team at the rally/match to be held on (date) at
(venue). Will you please sign the permission slip below if
you agree to your child attending.

The rally/match will finish at approximately (time). Your
child will need to be collected from school/venue. If there
is any problem with this arrangement please contact the
school as soon as possible.

                          Yours sincerely,

                          ................
- - - - - - - - - - - - - - - - - - - - - - - - - - - - - -
I give my permission for .....................to attend
the rally/match at (venue) on (date).

In the event of cancellation I can be contacted on
........................................

My child will be collected by me/another parent/need
transport home. (Please delete as applicable).

                     Signed...........................
```

You will need to take to the rally/match:

▷ order of play

▷ first aid kit

▷ whistle

▷ ball

▷ bibs/bands

▷ bin liners to sit on or to leave coats on etc.

▷ orange squash

▷ biscuits

The last two are important especially if the match/rally is after school. It may be several hours before the children have their tea and they may need something light to eat and drink to sustain them.

Many schools provide sports kit for their school teams. Parents usually wash the kit and return it to school. To make sure that none goes astray number the kit and keep a record of who takes which article. Fourth year juniors are very good at this type of organisation if you are too rushed to do it yourself.

Sports Day

There are so many different ways of organising a sports day it is impossible to deal with them all satisfactorily in this book. Most schools will have their own sports day traditions and favourite races. Here are a few suggestions if new ideas are needed:

1 Decide on the date of the Sports Day and an alternative date if the weather is bad. Tell the groundsmen of your two dates so they can mark out the tracks.

2 Appoint/ask for volunteers for the following posts:

▷ **Clerk of the Course:** Arranges programme of races and apparatus etc.

▷ **Marshalls:** Keep competitors and spectators under control and make sure that children are ready for their races.

▷ **Programme Steward:** Arranges printing and distribution of programme.

▷ **Starter:** Blows whistle (a starting gun is usually too loud for small children) to begin races.

▷ **Place Judges:** Give children a coloured or numbered card with their position in the race which they then take to the *recorders*.

▷ **Recorders:** These make a note of children's positions and teams and any times if these are kept. They also keep score and work out the winning team(s).

▷ **Time keepers:** To time events if records are kept.

▷ **Judges:** For field events.

▷ **Helpers:** To rake sand, put out obstacle course etc.

▷ **A V.I.P:** To award prizes.

▷ **Tea-ladies:** to organise refreshments for the spectators and competitors.

Equipment

You may need:

- ▷ whistle/starting pistol
- ▷ tape/posts/chairs etc. to cordon off area for competitors
- ▷ finishing tape
- ▷ rake (for sand for long and high jumps)
- ▷ competitors numbers/teams
- ▷ coloured bands
- ▷ placecards/numbers
- ▷ chalkboard and easel (chalk and duster)
- ▷ chairs for spectators
- ▷ first-aid equipment

and for the races:

- ▷ batons
- ▷ skipping ropes
- ▷ wellies!
- ▷ sacks
- ▷ spoons and eggs (plaster of Paris are a lot easier than boiled)
- ▷ obstacle race equipment

Choosing Teams

This really depends on whether the sports day is a serious competitive afternoon or a fun afternoon that all join in, or a mixture of both.

If the afternoon is seriously competitive then heats will need to be run to ascertain the competitors.

If the afternoon is mainly for the fun of joining in then teams will have to be arranged so that every child is able to compete and the races are not all suited to the athletic.

Most schools organise their Sports Days with the children in teams and have a mixture of serious events (i.e. sprints and relays) and not-so-serious (i.e. wellie and egg and spoon races). If the races are organised on a team basis then every child can have a go at everything and faster children will make up for the non-athletic who may feel ill at ease if they are racing as an individual.

The Events

Serious	**Not-so Serious**
Sprints (length suited to age of child)	Sack
	Wellie
Relay	Egg and Spoon
High Jump	Late for School
Triple Jump	
Throwing the cricket/rounders ball	

▷ **Wellie Race:**   Children race wearing extra-large wellingtons

▷ **Late for School:**   Children race along track having to put on various items of clothing and finally eat a piece of bread and butter (breakfast).

▷ **Chain Relay:**   Children are in teams of four. The first child runs down the track and collects the second child. While holding hands they both run back down the track to collect the third child and then all three children, still holding hands collect the fourth child. All four children run back down the track to the finish. Usually only a short piece of the track is used and it is wise to train the children to hold hands so that they are all facing the same direction or one poor child has to run backwards and may fall.

▷ **Tunnel Ball:**   Children stand in teams in a line with their feet apart. The first child rolls a netball between his legs to the second child who pushes it on to the third child. When the ball reaches the last child in the team he runs to the front and begins again. The first team to have the first child back at the front wins.

▷ **Team Hoop-la:**   Children stand in a line holding hands. End child has a large hoop in his hand. The children have to pass the hoop down the line so that each child has passed through it with out breaking their hand hold. The children must also stay in a line so the spare hands of the end children are not used. The trick is that the first child steps into the hoop and then it passes over his head onto the head of the next child who steps out of it so that the next child can step into it.

▷ **Beanbag in Bucket:**   Beanbags and buckets are arranged as shown.

Child has to pick up beanbag 'A' and put it in the bucket. Then he does the same, one at a time, with the other beanbags. He then runs to the finishing line.

With all team games it is easier to see who has won if the children are taught to sit down when they have finished. If the ground is wet they can crouch. However you must be strict and ensure that they only sit when the first child is in position back at the front of the line.

School Fetes and Bazaars

Many schools have a school fete or bazaar to raise money for much needed equipment for the school. The fete can be organised by the staff or by the PTA.

Obviously the organisation of such an event is very hard work, especially if you are new, so here are a few ideas to make things a little easier.

Things to sort out in advance:

1 Place for event to be held (including wet weather venue if necessary), time and date.

2 List of sideshows and stalls, including person responsible for running/organising.

3 Publicity. You will need to put the advertisement in your local paper in good time. Prepare posters and handouts and let your local radio station know.

4 Prizes. Some one brave will have to approach local businesses to ask for suitable donations as prizes. Small prizes may have to be bought for lucky dips etc.

5 A public address system, music and the wherewithall to power it.

6 Supporting attractions. Ask any local groups if they would like to appear and show their skills. Such groups may include:

   ▷ The Armed Services

   ▷ The Fire and Ambulance Services

   ▷ The Police

   ▷ Morris Dancers

   ▷ Drum Majorettes or Marching Band

   ▷ Hand-bell Ringers

   ▷ Dance Groups

   ▷ Gymnastic Clubs

   ▷ Model Aircraft Clubs

Don't forget your own children can give demonstrations of:

   ▷ Country dancing

   ▷ Maypole dancing

   ▷ Gymnastics etc.

This will ensure that at least these children (and their families) will attend the fete.

7 Refreshments. You will need not only the food but a tea urn (and a power socket), tables and chairs, cutlery and crockery.

8 Bunting, signs and posters for each stall.

9 First-aid arrangements.

10 Disposal of rubbish.

It helps to relieve the pressure on the organisers if that great untapped resource of labour — the children — are used to help. They usually love it and gain educationally from it as well. Ask each class to provide a stall/sideshow and ask the children for volunteers to be in charge of it. Make sure you have their parents' permission and have a rota, your helpers will also want to look around at some time.

Easy stalls/sideshows for the children to run/organise include:

   ▷ **Cake Stall**

   ▷ **Bottle stall**

▷ **Tombola**

▷ **Guess weight/name of something**

▷ **Marble Competition**   How many marbles can you get into a jar using a tablespoon in one minute?

▷ **Peg Competition**   How many clothes pegs can you take off a washing line using only one hand?

▷ **Egg Competition**   Collect empty eggshells which still retain their shape. Half bury these and half a dozen whole eggs (preferably hard boiled) in a tray of sand/sawdust so that they all look whole. Competitors pay a small sum to pick out three eggs. If they choose a whole egg, they win a small prize.

▷ **Treasure Hunt**   Copy a map of the local area, or get the children to draw a map of an imaginative place e.g. a desert island. Divide into squares. Organiser chooses one square for location of treasure and seals information in an envelope. Competitors pay a small sum to choose a square.

▷ **Clock Watch**   Headteacher winds up a clock and seals it in the school safe about two days before fete. Competitors have to guess at what time the clock will have stopped.

▷ **Anything sponsored**
    ▷ skipping

    ▷ running

    ▷ swimming

    ▷ spelling

    ▷ reading

    ▷ growing a plant from seed (and then selling it at the fete!)

    ▷ bouncing: there are many companies who provide an inflatable castle/ dragon etc. for a sponsored bounce. One such company is: Mr Bounce Inflatable Play Equipment P.O. Box 44 Leamington Spa Warwickshire CV31 3QU Tel. 0926 38587

▷ **Car Washing**   This needs adult supervision but with a well-trained group of older children it can be very profitable. You can't really fail with this one because having done one car you may find that clients will give you a donation NOT to clean their car!

▷ **Programmes**   Use an art lesson to get the children to design a programme (so you'll sell at least one to the successful designer's family). If the programme has a lucky number parents can sell them to friends and neighbours who are not coming to the fete on a raffle ticket basis. It helps if there is a returnable strip where the purchasers of the programme write their name and address. These strips can be placed in a tub from which the winner can be drawn at the fete.

▷ **Second-Hand Books and Toys**   This is very popular with children as they donate (with sighs of relief from parents) their old toys and buy their friends' old toys instead.

On The Day

Arrange helpers to arrive early to set out the stalls and side shows. These will look more festive if covered with fabric — curtains or tablecloths will do.

If you are using chairs and tables from more than one classroom, make sure that they are named/numbered or you may find you have mysteriously lost your new tables to another classroom.

Stalls and sideshows will need a float and may require more change as the afternoon progresses.

STALL	Float						Total Received	PROFIT TOTAL
Tombola	£2	change £5	Received £10	change £2			Received £21	£22
Guess the weight of the cake	£2	change £1	change £0.50	change £2			£15	£9.50
Raffle	£2						£36	£34
Toys & Books	£2	change £2	Received £5				£12	£13

It helps if the person acting as treasurer is in the same place all afternoon should more change be required or large sums of money need to be deposited.

Older children can wander round with some competitions such as 'Guess the Weight of the Cake' or 'Guess the name of the Doll'.

If the attractions involving the children are held at intervals throughout the afternoon you are guaranteed a captive audience of parents waiting to see their offspring perform!

Clearing up should not be a problem if all the helpers know where to return tables etc. Large bin liners are useful for rubbish and unsold items which you may wish to keep for the next jumble sale.

School Pets

Animals in school provide a twofold educational experience. They can be used as a basis for scientific study and to teach the child respect and care for all living things. Most primary schools will have some animal as a school pet and would not dream of using their class hamster as part of a scientific experiment. He is there to be loved and looked after and scientific investigation will probably stop at measuring his rate of growth. Other animals may be introduced to the classroom environment either by chance, e.g. house martins may make a nest in the eaves of the school building, or because of the class topic e.g. tadpoles for a topic on ponds.

Before you dash out to buy a cuddly baby rabbit as a sound educational experience for your children, there are a few things you need to consider. Firstly there is the legal aspect of keeping animals in captivity.

1 You are not allowed to cause any animal unnecessary suffering or abuse or to neglect it. Are you sure your children will look after it properly?

2 You are not allowed to abandon an animal in circumstances likely to cause it unnecessary suffering. This could have implications when asking children to take animals home for the holidays.

3 It is illegal to sell animals without a petshop licence and to sell animals to children under the age of twelve years. This could have implications if you wish to find homes for your baby rabbits or gerbils.

4 Schools are not allowed to have any live badger, dead badger or part of a badger.

5 You are not allowed to keep scheduled wild animals without a licence from the local authority. Some are offered for sale by licensed pet suppliers or may be brought into school by children whose parents may hold a licence to keep them. It is illegal if they are brought into school.

6 You may not take wild birds, their eggs or their nests (while in use). You may not keep a bird in a cage unless it has enough room to stretch its wings freely. Some birds if kept in captivity must be ringed.

7 No protected animal may be killed, injured or taken. You may bring them into school for observation if you are licensed to do so. This does not apply to adders which are covered by the Dangerous Wild Animals Act 1976. Some animals have full protection which includes spawn and tadpoles. If a child brings one of

these species into school you should gently explain why you cannot keep it and return it as soon as possible to the place where it was found.

8 You may not disturb certain protected species or their shelter or resting places.

9 You may not capture shrews without a licence. If you wish to capture other small mammals you may use a Longworth trap with a 13 mm shrew escape hole in the side.

10 If you keep any farm animals you will have to comply with all legislation dealing with the keeping of livestock.

11 You may not uproot any wild flower unless it is on your own land or you have permission.

12 You may not pick, uproot, destroy or collect seeds from any protected plants.

This may all seem far removed from the class gerbil but many schools use their local environment for ecological study and many of the protected birds, plants and animals may be found close to the school. These include certain species of owls, bats, butterflies, amphibians (including the common frog), lizards, snails, snakes and dormice, otters and slow-worms. The full list is given in the appendix.

More detailed guidance on the legal aspects of keeping animals in school can be found in 'Animals and Plants in Schools: Legal Aspects Administrative Memorandum No 1/89' from the Department of Education and Science. Your Headteacher should have a copy — somewhere. In Appendices on p151–p152 there are some lists of protected species.

Secondly, you need consider what type of animal you wish to have, where it is going to live and who is going to be responsible for it. To help you here is a list of the most common animals to be found in schools.

The Hamster

An endearing little rodent which is usually safe with children. The main problem with hamsters is that they will sleep for most of the school day only becoming active in the afternoon. They also tend to smell quite strongly. Hamsters also have a short life span (the maximum life span is about two years). This can be an advantage or a disadvantage depending on your views and the character of your hamster. It is distressing for children when their class hamster dies but a situation like this does help them to come to terms with the concept of mortality and in dealing with bereavement.

Hamsters should be kept singly in cages or they will fight. If you wish to breed hamsters the male should be removed from the cage after mating.

Home

A hamster will need a large draught-proof cage, which should also be gnaw-proof. The cage should have a sleeping area and room for the animal to exercise. If you have a wheel it should be solid and attached to the cage so that the hamster cannot become trapped in it. The hamster will also need something to gnaw — a cotton reel, dog biscuit, peach stone or peg is ideal. The bottom of the cage should be covered in sawdust or something similar to absorb waste. If possible this should be deep enough to allow the animal to burrow.

The hamster will also need a water bottle. Hamsters will usually tip over water containers but a heavy container will be suitable for food. The hamster will probably remove the food to its store. Try not to disturb its food store but check regularly to see if the food is going mouldy.

Feeding

Hamsters can be fed on a mix obtainable from pet food suppliers. This can be supplemented with any seeds or nuts, porridge oats, wholemeal bread or puppy meal. The hamster may also enjoy fresh fruit and vegetables and some wild plants such as dandelion or clover.

Care

The cage will need to be cleaned out at least once a week. It should washed with warm soapy water and dried thoroughly. Bedding and sawdust should be replaced. The hamster will need to be housed in some temporary, gnaw-proof accommodation while this is going on. In a school there should be no shortage of volunteers to clean out a small pet and it is easier if the children clean out their pet in small groups. Two children to deal with the cage and two to look after the hamster. If you wish to have a rota, make sure that someone from the previous week who knows how to do the task teaches the new group. In this way you will not have to repeat yourself eight times and they will extend their language skills.

However, children tend to be over enthusiastic and you will probably need to supervise them at least for the first few times the hamster is cleaned out to make sure that they do not use the staff tea-towel for drying the cage and that they do not bury the hamster in sawdust.

Hamsters can be very friendly little animals and love to explore. If you buy a baby hamster you will have to teach the children the correct way to handle it and explain that the new hamster is nervous so it will have to get used to them. If you do not do this and allow twenty children to pass around one frightened baby hamster, it is possible that it will bite someone. You will then have a terrified child and a terrified hamster neither accomplishing the educational aims you set out to achieve in owning the hamster in the first place.

I try to explain to the children how big the world must look to small animals. Showing them illustrations from stories dealing with giants usually gives them the general idea. We then talk about how big the children must look to the hamster. This leads nicely on to how frightening it must be for the hamster to have a large hand bearing down on it and how much nicer it is for the hamster if it is picked up from underneath, having run onto the hand first. Before hamsters can be picked up using this scooping method the children will need to leave their hands in the cage so that the new hamster becomes used to the texture and smell of a human hand. Food in the palm of the hand helps. This method also helps the nervous child who has never handled a small pet before become used to the feel of the pet in their hand. If this is not done and the child is just given the pet to hold he may panic and drop the pet.

Another subject which I discuss with the children is poking their fingers through the bars of the cage. I ask the children to hold the tip of one finger with their other hand. Then I ask them what their finger tip must look like to the hamster. Someone usually guesses a peanut, eventually. What do hamsters do to peanuts? Yes, they eat them. So what is the hamster likely to do to your finger? Bite it, very good. If a child is foolish enough to be bitten after this explanation, I make it clear that all sympathy (and possible medical treatment!) will go to the hamster.

Mice and Rats

Mice are less lovable in appearance than hamsters and many people do not like their very quick way of moving. Also unpopular are their long tails but they are very clean animals and make excellent pets. Rats are very intelligent and with patience can be trained.

Mice are usually quite timid but are easy to tame. Try not to put male and female mice together as they breed very easily. But animals of the same sex can be kept together — if the cage is large enough.

Feeding

A food mix for mice and rats can be bought at most pet shops. This can be supplemented with fresh greens and apple or carrot. They need to be fed little and often.

Home

A cage suitable for a hamster may also be suitable for a mouse. Rats need a cage three to four times this size. If buying a cage with bars, make sure that they are narrow enough to prevent the mice escaping. Mice can also be kept in an aquarium with a fine wire mesh over the top. This home has the advantage that the mice are able to burrow.

Care

Mice will need to be cleaned out about two or three times a week. Much of the advice given for hamsters will also apply to mice and rats especially in relation to cleaning out and handling. Mice love to play and will need a solid wheel to prevent their tails and paws from becoming trapped. They also enjoy playing with cardboard tubes and small boxes with holes cut in the sides.

Gerbils

Gerbils are very popular school pets because they are active during the day. They are friendly little animals which do not have the strong smell associated with hamsters. Gerbils of the same sex will live together happily. The major drawback with gerbils is that they suffer with the same problem as rats and mice — they have a long scaly tail which many people find off-putting.

Feeding

A mix suitable for gerbils is available from most pet shops. They need a dry mixture of grains e.g. maize, barley and wheat. You can supplement this with sunflower seeds and a small amount of fresh greens. Stale food should be removed daily.

Home

Although gerbils can be kept in a cage suitable for a hamster or mouse they are happier in an aquarium with a wire mesh lid. The aquarium should be about two thirds full of some suitable burrowing material for example peat, potting compost, soil straw or a mixture of these.

Bedding suitable for a hamster or mice should also be given. They will also need a heavy dish for food and a pet's water bottle.

Care

The burrowing material will need to be changed about every three months. Gerbils do not drink very much so you will need to change their water frequently to prevent it from going stale. Gerbils will take food with their front paws from a human hand and this is one way of taming them. They can be picked up using the method already described for hamsters but when holding a gerbil, cup your other hand over the gerbil to prevent it from jumping out of your hand. It is a good idea for children to hold the gerbil on the floor or over a table (you could put a cloth on the table for extra padding), so that if the gerbil did jump out of a child's hand it would not harm itself.

Never pick up a gerbil by its tail. It has a defence mechanism whereby, if trapped by the tail, the outer skin will come off so that the gerbil can escape. If you see your gerbil with bone where his tail should be, this is what has happened and he will need to go to the vet for treatment.

Rabbits

Rabbits are very popular school pets and children relate to them well. However, not all rabbits relate well to children so you need to be very careful who handles and cleans out your rabbit unless it is of a very soppy temperament.

Rabbits are sociable, and animals of the same sex will live together. Rabbits will also live happily with guinea pigs.

Feeding

Rabbit food can be bought at most pet shops. This can be supplemented with fresh greens and carrots. Rabbits will also need fresh hay every day preferably in a rack to keep it clean. Rabbits can also be given their food mashed with warm or cold water or a mash made with milk and wholemeal bread.

Home

Rabbits are usually kept outside in a hutch. In the winter they may need to be brought inside. Many people use their garage. There may not be facilities at school for you to be able to do this although a shed would be suitable.

The rabbit hutch will also need to be kept somewhere where it can be moved into the shade during the summer.

Rabbit hutches need to be of a suitable size (the RSPCA recommend a minimum hutch size of 150 cm × 60 cm × 60 cm for two small or medium rabbits) and divided into two areas. The sleeping area should have a solid door and hay should be provided as bedding. The living area should be large enough for the rabbit to move around easily and the floor should be covered with sawdust or cat litter. The rabbit will also need a heavy food dish, a water bottle and a log to gnaw. The door to the living area should be of wire netting.

The hutch must be raised from the ground to keep out damp and other animals.

The best arrangement for a rabbit is to allow it freedom in an enclosed space. This area will have to be securely fenced off. The fencing must be sunk well into the ground to prevent the rabbit escaping by burrowing. At night the rabbit must be shut securely back in its hutch.

If this arrangement is impossible then your rabbit will need a run. Again, this needs to be secure so that the rabbit cannot escape by burrowing and the run will need to be moved regularly.

The hutch will need to be cleaned out at least once a week and feeding dishes will need to be washed every day. The bedding and litter or sawdust will need to be replaced and the hutch washed with warm soapy water and dried thoroughly. You will need to have alternative accommodation for your rabbit while the hutch is being cleaned.

If your rabbit is to become tame it will need to be handled frequently. Rabbits tend to be nervous creatures and a struggling rabbit can be too strong for a young child to handle. Never pick up a rabbit by its ears. Rabbits are best held close against the body with the child's arms taking the weight of the animal. Train the children to take the rabbit in and out of the hutch with its back towards them so that the powerful hind legs are not in a position to kick or scratch.

Guinea Pigs

These lovable little animals are not found in schools as often as rabbits perhaps because they have the reputation for being nervous. Guinea pigs are best kept in pairs or family groups with the males removed. They are also happy living with rabbits although they are less hardy.

Feeding

Guinea pigs need a diet containing high amounts of vitamin C. One meal can be a pet food mix for rabbits or a cereal mash made with milk. The mash made with milk and wholemeal bread is also suitable for guinea pigs. Their second meal will need to be fresh vegetables and fruit. They will also need hay every day. The hay should be in a rack to prevent it from becoming soiled. Guinea pigs can also be given wild plants such as clover and dandelion.

Home

Guinea pigs can be kept in a rabbit hutch. They will also need sleeping and living compartments. The sleeping compartment should have hay for bedding and there should be a layer of sawdust or litter on the floor of the living compartment. They will also need a heavy feeding dish and a water bottle. The hutch must be positioned off the ground and out of draughts and strong sunlight. In winter guinea pigs really need to be brought indoors. A large airy shed is suitable.

Guinea pigs need to be cleaned out more often than rabbits. The hutch will need to be cleaned out every day. The hay and litter should be replaced as needed. The hutch should also be washed out regularly with soap and water.

Guinea pigs do not burrow so their run does not have to have wire mesh underneath but it does need to be sturdy so that they cannot escape by crawling underneath.

Care

Guinea pigs are heavy animals for their size and need to be supported by two hands. They tend to be rather timid at first but with patience they usually come to enjoy being stroked and handled.

Long haired guinea pigs will need grooming every day.

If your hamster, mouse or rat escapes from its cage and is loose somewhere in your classroom it is unlikely that you will find it to catch with all the children helping you. Wait until all the children have gone home, put some food in the middle of the floor and listen. Often in the silent classroom you can hear the animal moving. If you see the escapee, you will be very fortunate to catch it with your hands and in trying to catch it in an upturned basin you may cause it injury. Try dropping a large piece of cloth over the animal. Sometimes this causes them to freeze and you can then gently scoop it up in the piece of fabric.

An easier alternative to the above is to rest a jam jar at an angle (open end uppermost) against some books. Place a small amount of food in the bottom and leave the room for a short time. If the animal goes into the jam jar for the food it will be trapped.

The aforementioned animals are usually kept in school as pets and although their growth may be studied or a play area made for them, their main purpose in the classroom is to teach children respect and responsibility towards other living things. You may wish to keep other animals in the classroom in order that the children may study them more scientifically. Here are brief details of the most common.

Earthworms

These can be kept in any large container filled with damp soil. An infant sand tray will do. An interesting experiment is to divide the container into four portions as shown:

The container will need to be kept covered.

A certain number of worms are put into the middle of the tray and a week later the number of worms in each area are counted. Do make sure that the worms are counted carefully. The children become very upset if it appears that some of the worms have escaped and if you have more worms than you started with you will have a very hard time convincing them that the worms have not had babies!

A variation on this experiment is to fill the container with moist soil and add some worms. Collect some dead leaves and lay these over the top of the soil. Then cover everything and leave it for about a week. The result should be a clear demonstration of how worms aid the formation of soil.

You may wish to study the movements of worms. In this case you will need to build a wormery. This can be as simple or as complicated as you like. A very simple wormery can be built as shown:

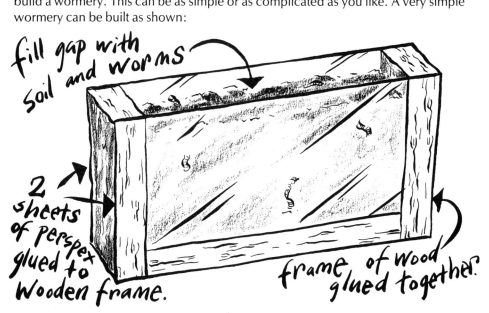

Don't forget to leave some leaves on the top for food.

Ants

The hustle and bustle of ants can be fascinating to study in the classroom. Ants can be kept in a similar construction to the wormery so that their nest can be studied. An alternative to this could be an aquarium with a lid. If you find an ants' nest try to collect as many ants as possible with a spade and bring back to school in a sealed container. Put the contents of the ants' nest into your glass container and if you are fortunate to have captured the queen, the ants will quickly organise themselves in their new home.

The ants' home will need to be kept moist and they will need to be fed on sweet sugary substances, insects and meat.

Water Life

Goldfish are often kept in schools because they are fairly easy to look after and may be therapeutic for the teacher! However, you may wish to keep other forms of aquatic life to study. It is not advisable to put these into the same fish tank that houses your goldfish.

If you wish to study the myriad of small inhabitants in our ponds you will need a tank suitable for fish and some pond water and weed. The simplest arrangement is to collect a bucket of pond water, pour it into your tank and study the wildlife you are certain to have collected. You must have some plant life to oxygenate the water and to provide food for the herbivorous wild life. Do not collect pond animals with a net and put them straight into tap water. Tap water is only suitable for wildlife once it has been left for at least a day or two.

A more interesting idea is to build your own pond. With the destruction of so many natural ponds much of our aquatic wildlife is now to be found surviving in garden and ornamental ponds. A school pond could be an important addition to the ecology of your area as well as providing first hand experience for the children.

Unambitious ponds are fairly simple to build especially with a class full of willing workers. The building of the pond could also use mathematical and mapping skills. Although there are various grades of pond liners, try to go for the most expensive the school can afford. Plastic sheeting is not really suitable as the plastic will harden in strong sunlight and then split.

Building a Simple Pond

1 Contact your local education authority for any regulations they may have over ponds in school grounds. Ponds are potentially hazardous and may need to be fenced off or only built to a certain depth.

2 Choose your site. This needs to be sunny and not overshadowed by trees. For wildlife an ideal setting would be facing south-west.

3 Choose your shape. A shallow saucer shape is the easiest. The sides need to slope very gently but the depth needs to be at least 60 cm to prevent the pond from freezing completely in the winter.

4 Dig your hole. Remember to dig the hole slightly larger than your design to allow for padding etc. There should be no sharp corners in your design. They would be difficult for the pond liner to cover and may eventually cause the liner to split. Remove a layer of soil from edge of the hole to a depth of about 5 cm and back to about 30 cm.

5 Remove all sharp objects from the sides and bottom of the hole.

6 Line your hole with soft padding — sand, newspapers, old pieces of carpet are ideal.

7 Spread your liner over the hole. Weight down the edges with bricks — or children.

8 Gently lower the liner down so that it covers the hole. If you have to stand on the liner in the hole, put some padding such as newspaper under your feet. Scatter some soil to cover the bottom of the liner. In this soil you will be growing your pond plants. You do not need to make this layer very thick.

9 Through a garden hose gently run water into your pond until the liner is full. If you are too vigorous you will stir up the soil in the bottom and have a mud bath instead of a pond.

10 While the pond is being filled put back the soil you removed from the edge of the hole. This is now used to hold down the edge of the pond liner and to merge the edge of the pond with the edge of soil so that you have a wetlands area.

11 Buy or acquire some oxygenating plants. These need to be firmly anchored to the bottom so that they grow in the soil you have thoughtfully provided and not float around on the surface of the water. Plants that have been donated from friends or parents with ponds are ideal because as they pull them out you will probably be given some minibeasts to inhabit your pond as well. Try to buy native species of water plants as this will encourage the wildlife you wish to inhabit your pond.

12 Leave the pond for several weeks before introducing any donated wildlife — snails etc. You will be surprised at how quickly the pond will be colonised by various insect species.

If you are lucky your pond will soon be teeming with wildlife and you may even be fortunate enough to provide a habitat for some of our more endangered species such as frogs and newts.

Caterpillars and Insects

An easy makeshift home for most species of insects can be made from a fish tank with a close-mesh wire lid (or side if you wish to turn the fish tank onto its side). Put a layer of soil in the bottom and some plants if possible. If collecting caterpillars, make a note on which plant they were found so that you can collect some more leaves for them for food.

Make the habitat in the aquarium as much like the natural habitat of the insect as possible. If the insect is a woodland floor animal you will need to keep the cage moist and in shade. You will also need to provide items such as dead leaves and some dead wood and bark. If the insect comes from a dry, sunny habitat you will need to include some branches, some dry leaves, some twigs with leaves on etc.

It is good hygiene to teach the children to wash their hands after handling any animals. Children should not put their hands in pond water if they have cuts or open wounds on them.

All the information given in this chapter is intended for general guidance only. The responsibility for the welfare of any animal in the classroom rests with the teacher and no animal should be allowed to suffer through ignorance or neglect. Children usually respond well to wildlife in the classroom and will follow the example of their teacher. Don't keep spiders or snakes if you are absolutely terrified of them. The children will recognise your fear and be trained to fear the animals themselves.

Appendices

Curriculum vitae

<u>Curriculum vitae</u>

```
Name Mrs Ann Teacher        Date of Birth    12.3.60
     (nee Student)          Nat.Ins. No.     XY 12 34 56 Z
                            D.E.S. Ref.      78/12345

Home Address:  Church Cottage,
               Old Lane,
               Anyville,
               Heathshire,
               HE2 4RZ

Telephone No.  0843 7654
```

<u>Qualifications</u>

Cambridge Local Examination Syndicate

```
'O' Levels:     June 1975     English Literature     History
                              English language       French
                              Mathematics            Art
                              Physics                Chemistry

'A' Levels:     June 1978     Physics
                              Chemistry
                              Mathematics

Degree:         Anytown University
                June 1982     Mathematics B. Ed.
```

<u>Education</u>

```
Secondary School:  Sept 1971-July 1978 Heathtown School,
                                       School Road,
                                       Heathtown,
                                       Heathshire.

College:           Sept 1978-July 1982 Anytown College,
                                       College RD.
                                       Anytown,
                                       Heathshire.
```

```
College Courses:        Age Range:          Junior 7-11 years
                        Main Subject:       Mathematics
                        Secondary Subject:  Music
                        General Subjects:   Education, Language, PE,
                                            Art and Craft, Music,
                                            Science, RE.

Teaching Practices: King's Junior School, Anytown.
                    St. Peter's Middle School, Anytown.
                    Anyville Primary School, Anytown.
```

Previous Posts

```
Sept 1982-July 1983 St. Mark's Junior School
                    Heathtown

                    Heathshire LEA
                    Group 4 Junior School

Subjects Taught:    General Subjects to a second year class
                    (8-9 yrs).

Extra-Curricular
Activities:         Netball Practices, Chess Club.


Sept 1983-July 1986 Heathtown Primary School
                    Heathtown

                    Heathshire LEA
                    Group 2 Primary School
Subjects Taught:    General Subjects to all ages

Extra-Curricular
Activities:         Netball Practices, Chess Club, Drama Group.
```

Courses

```
Children with Special Needs  Feb 1983
Art and Craft Techniques May 1983
Handwriting                  Nov 1984
PE in the Primary School May/June 1985
Netball Umpiring             Oct 1986
```

Oral

discussion
instructions
    – giving
    – receiving
role play
reading aloud
use of a/v aids
sound patterns &
  rhythms
choral speaking
lecturettes

Written

imaginative
factual
instructions
        – giving
        – receiving
letters
    – informal
    – formal
descriptive
note–taking

LANGUAGE SKILLS

Grammar and Punctuation

capital letters
full stops
sentences
commas
question mark
exclamation mark
vowels/consonants
nouns
        – proper
        – common
verbs
adjectives
adverbs
pronouns
tenses
conjunctions
singular & plural
prepositions
subject/object
direct speech
indirect speech
quotation marks
paragraphs
abbreviations
similies
metaphors
alliteration
onomatopoeia

Reading

fiction of all kinds
poetry
plays
for comprehension
dictionary skills
using encyclopaedias
non–fiction
instructions
fun, game &
  puzzle books
cloze passages
phonic skills
silent reading
group reading
reading aloud
being read to
reading other
  children's work
reading games
experiences to
  stimulate reading
talking about and
  investigating books

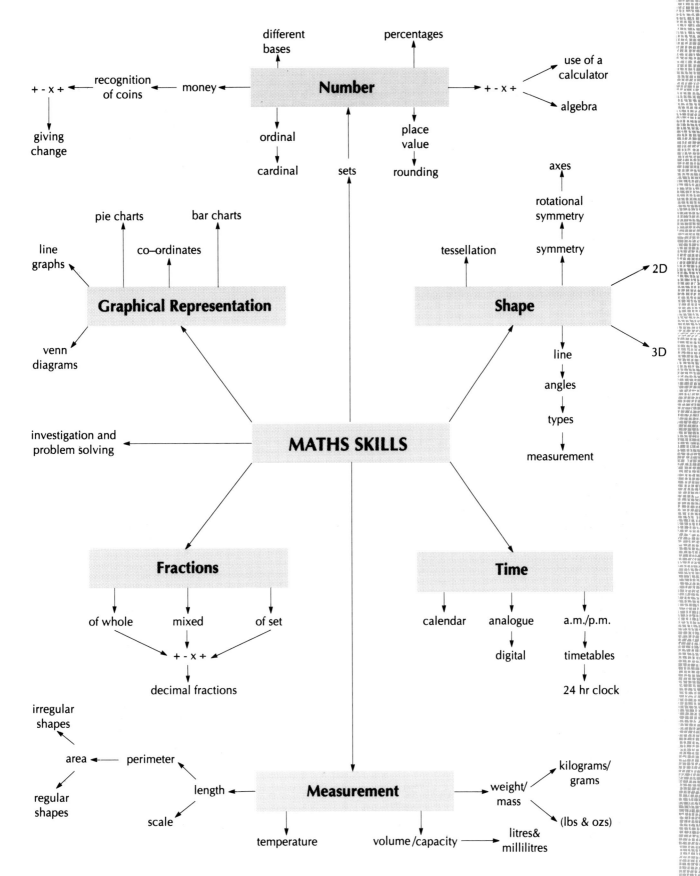

ART SKILLS

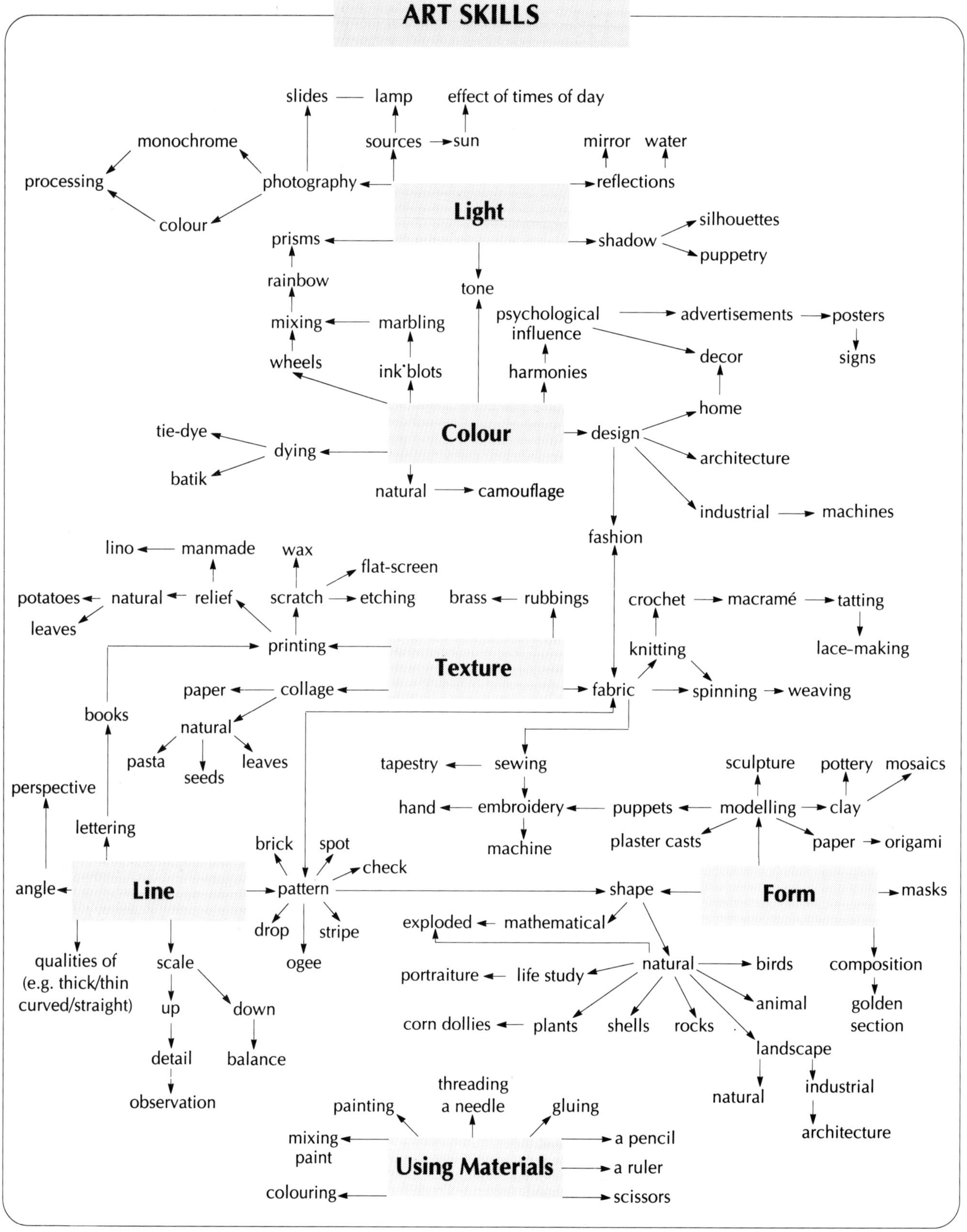

Light

slides — lamp   effect of times of day

sources → sun

monochrome   mirror   water

processing   photography ←   → reflections

colour

prisms ←   → shadow → silhouettes
→ puppetry

rainbow   tone

mixing ← marbling   psychological influence → advertisements → posters

wheels   ink blots   harmonies   → decor → signs

Colour   → design → home

tie-dye   → architecture

dying ←   batik   → industrial → machines

natural → camouflage   fashion

lino ← manmade   wax

potatoes ← natural ← relief   scratch → flat-screen   brass ← rubbings   crochet → macramé → tatting

leaves   → etching   knitting   lace-making

printing ←   **Texture**   → fabric → spinning → weaving

paper ← collage ←

books   natural

pasta   seeds   leaves   tapestry ← sewing   sculpture   pottery   mosaics

perspective   hand   embroidery ← puppets ← modelling → clay

lettering   brick   spot   machine   plaster casts   paper → origami

angle ←   **Line** → pattern → check   → shape ←   **Form** → masks

drop   stripe   exploded ← mathematical   composition

qualities of   scale   ogee   portraiture ← life study   natural → birds   golden section

(e.g. thick/thin   up   down   corn dollies ← plants   shells   rocks   animal

curved/straight)   detail   balance   landscape   industrial

observation   threading   natural   architecture

painting   a needle   gluing

mixing   → a pencil

paint   **Using Materials** → a ruler

colouring ←   → scissors

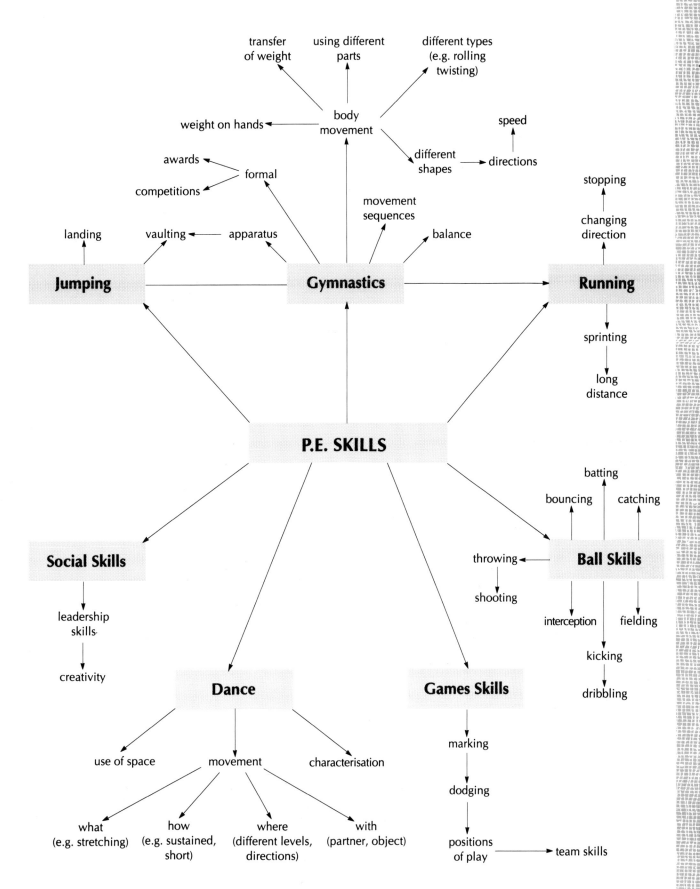

List of the 100 most used words in the English Language

a	and	he	I	in	is	it	of
that	the	to	was				

all	are	as	at	be	but	for	had
have	him	his	not	on	one	said	so
they	we	with	you				

about	an	back	been	before	big	by	call
came	can	come	could	did	do	down	first
from	get	go	has	her	here	if	into
just	like	little	look	made	make	me	more
much	must	my	new	no	now	off	old
only	or	other	our	out	over	right	see
she	some	their	them	then	there	this	two
up	want	well	went	were	what	when	where
which	who	will	your				

Phonic Checksheet

Letters

a b c d e f g h
i j k l m n o p
q r s t u v w x
y z

Short Internal Vowel Sounds

—a—   —e—   —i—   —o—   —u—

Consonant Digraphs

ch gh ph qu sh th wh tch
shr thr sch

Initial Consonant Blends

bl br cl cr dr dw fl fr
gl gr pl pr sc sk sl sm
sn sp st sw tr tw scr shr
spl spr squ str thr

Final Consonant Blends

ld lp lt mp nch nd ng nk
nt sk sp st

Magic/Silent/Lazy e

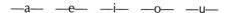

a—e e—e i—e o—e u—e

148

Vowel Digraphs

ai   ar   au   aw   ay   ea   ee   er
ew   ie   ir   oa   oe   oi   oo   or
ou   ow   oy   ue   ur

Silent Letters

b   g   gh   h   k   l   t   u
w

Endings

ation   ble   cial   cian   cient   cious   cle   dle
ed   er   est   es   fle   ge   gle   ing
ion   kle   ly   ple   re   sion   sle   tial
tient   tion tious tle   ture   ue   ure   y

Other Rules

Q and u always go together
Hard/soft c and g
Drop e before ing
Doubling letters to keep vowel short
Regular plurals end in s
F changes to v for the plural
Wor says were

LDA (for Aston Index and Goodenough draw-a-man IQ test)
LDA Duke Street, Wisbech, Cambs. PE13 2AE

The Daniels and Diack Spelling Test
[This is now out of print]

1 on	16 are	31 eye
2 hot	17 of	32 fight
3 cup	18 do	33 friend
4 van	19 who	34 done
5 jam	20 here	35 any
6 lost	21 ship	36 great
7 sit	22 food	37 sure
8 plan	23 fire	38 women
9 mud	24 thin	39 answer
10 beg	25 date	40 beautiful
11 the	26 chop	
12 go	27 seem	
13 for	28 dart	
14 so	29 loud	
15 me	30 form	

Scoring

1 5.2	11 6.2	21 7.3	31 8.7
2 5.3	12 6.3	22 7.5	32 9.0
3 5.4	13 6.4	23 7.6	33 9.2
4 5.5	14 6.5	24 7.7	34 9.5
5 5.6	15 6.6	25 7.8	35 9.8
6 5.7	16 6.7	26 7.9	36 10.2
7 5.8	17 6.8	27 8.1	37 10.5
8 5.9	18 7.0	28 8.2	38 11.0
9 6.0	19 7.1	29 8.3	39 11.6
10 6.1	20 7.2	30 8.5	40 12.3

Administering the Test

Give all the children a piece of paper and a pencil (or two). Explain that they are about to have a spelling test. They will have 40 words to write down (juniors like to know how long a test is, infants probably can't count that far!). Explain that you are going to say the word clearly. Then you are going to say the word in a sentence, because some words sound the same but are spelt differently and the sentence should make it clear which word you want. Then you are going to say the word again. If they do not understand the word, they must put up their hand and you will say the word again and put it in a different sentence. You will not be going back over any of the words but at half way and again at the end you will read out the list of words one more time.

The break at half way is a welcome rest for young children with a short concentration span.

With very young children the test can be discontinued when you feel they have passed the level of optimum performance.

Collect in and mark the papers. Their score can be transformed into a spelling age using the chart above. When dealing with competent spellers the jumps in spelling age are very large for answering an extra question correctly or incorrectly. It can look as if a child's spelling has improved or worsened dramatically in your mark book, but you will probably find that he has simply answered one question wrongly that he got correct last time.

For further information on Festivals

Religions through Festivals, general editor Clive Erricker, published by *Longman Group UK Limited*, is a very useful series.

Also, *Festivals in World Religions* produced by the Shap Working Party and published by *Longman Group UK Limited* is full of information. Alternatively, contact the Multicultural Education Resources Centre of your local Education Authority.

Protected birds

Part I

Wild Birds specially protected at all times

Avocet
Bee-eater
Bittern
Bittern, Little
Bluethroat
Brambling
Bunting, Cirl
Bunting, Lapland
Bunting, Snow
Buzzard, Honey
Chough
Corncrake
Crake, Spotted
Crossbills (all species)
Curlew, Stone
Divers (all species)
Dotterel
Duck, Long-tailed
Eagle, Golden
Eagle, White-tailed

Falcon, Gyr
Fieldfare
Firecrest
Garganey
Godwit, Black-tailed
Goshawk
Grebe, Black-necked
Grebe, Slavonian
Greenshank
Gull, Little
Gull, Mediterranean
Harriers (all species)
Heron, Purple
Hobby
Hoopoe
Kingfisher
Kite, Red
Merlin
Oriole, Golden
Osprey

Owl, Barn
Owl, Snowy
Peregrine
Petrel, Leach's
Phalarope, Red-necked
Plover, Kentish
Plover, Little Ringed
Quail, Common
Redstart, Black
Redwing
Rosefinch, Scarlet
Ruff
Sandpiper, Green
Sandpiper, Purple
Sandpiper, Wood
Scaup
Scoter, Common
Scoter, Velvet
Serin
Shorelark

Shrike, Red-backed
Spoonbill
Stilt, Black-winged
Stint, Temminck's
Swan, Bewick's
Swan, Whooper
Tern, Black
Tern, Little
Tern, Roseate
Tit, Bearded
Tit, Crested
Treecreeper, Short-toed
Warbler, Cetti's
Warbler, Dartford
Warbler, Marsh
Warbler, Savi's
Whimbrel
Woodlark
Wryneck

Part II

Wild Birds specially protected during the closed season

Goldeneye
Goose, Greylag (in Outer
  Hebrides, Caithness,
  Sutherland and Wester
  Ross only)
Pintail

Spoonbill
Stilt, Black-winged
Stint, Temminck's
Tern, Black
Tern, Little
Tern, Roseate

Tit, Bearded
Tit, Crested
Treecreeper, Short-toed
Warbler, Cetti's
Warbler, Dartford
Warbler, Marsh

Warbler, Savi's
Whimbrel
Woodlark
Wryneck

Animals which are protected

Adder
Anemone, Ivell's Sea
Anemone, Startlet Sea
Apus
Bats, Horseshoe (all species)
Bats, Typical (all species)
Beetle, Rainbow Leaf
Bettle, Violet Click
Burbot
Butterfly, Chequered Skipper
Butterfly, Heath Fritillary
Butterfly, Large Blue
Butterfly, Swallowtail
Cat, Wild
Cicada, New Forest
Cricket, Field

Cricket, Mole
Dolphin, Bottle-nosed
Dolphin, Common
Dormouse
Dragonfly, Norfolk Aeshna
Frog, Common
Grasshopper, Wart-biter
Leech, Medicinal
Lizard, Sand
Lizard, Viviparous
Marten, Pine
Mat, Trembling Sea
Moth, Barberry Carpet
Moth, Black-veined
Moth, Essex Emerald
Moth, New Forest Burnet

Moth, Reddish Buff
Moth, Viper's Bugloss
Newt, Great Crested
  (otherwise known as Warty
  newt)
Newt, Palmate
Newt, Smooth
Otter, Common
Porpoise, Harbour (otherwise
  known as Common
  porpoise)
Sandworm, Lagoon
Shrimp, Fairy
Shrimp, Lagoon Sand
Slow-worm
Snail, Carthusian

Snail, Glutinous
Snail, Sandbowl
Snake, Grass
Snake, Smooth
Spider, Fen Raft
Spider, Ladybird
Squirrel, Red
Toad, Common
Toad, Natterjack
Turtles, Marine (all species)
Vendace
Walrus
Whale (all species)
Whitefish

Animals which may not be killed or taken by certain methods

Badger
Bats, Horseshoe (all species)
Bats, Typical (all species)
Cat, Wild

Dolphin, Bottle-nosed
Dolphin, Common
Dormice (all species)
Hedgehog

Marten, Pine
Otter, Common
Polecat

Porpoise, Harbour (otherwise
  known as Common
  porpoise)
Shrews (all species)
Squirrel, Red

Plants which are protected

Adder's-tongue, Least
Alison, Small
Broomrape, Bedstraw
Broomrape, Oxtongue
Broomrape, Thistle
Cabbage, Lung
Calamint, Wood
Catchfly, Alpine
Cinquefoil, Rock
Club-rush, Triangular
Colt's-foot, Purple
Cotoneaster, Wild
Cottongrass, Slender
Cow-wheat, Field
Crocus, Sand
Cudweed, Jersey
Cudweed, Red-tipped
Diapensia
Eryngo, Field
Fern, Dickie's Bladder
Fern, Killarney
Fleabane, Alpine
Fleabane, Small
Galingale, Brown

Gentian, Alpine
Gentian, Fringed
Gentian, Spring
Germander, Cut-leaved
Germander, Water
Gladiolus, Wild
Goosefoot, Stinking
Grass-poly
Hare's-ear, Sickle-leaved
Hare's-ear, Small
Hawk's-beard, Stinking
Heath, Blue
Helleborine, Red
Helleborine, Young's
Horsetail, Branched
Hound's-tongue, Green
Knawel, Perennial
Knotgrass, Sea
Lady's-slipper

Lavender, Sea

Leek, Round-headed
Lettuce, Least
Lily, Snowdon

Marsh-mallow, Rough
Marshwort, Creeping
Milk-parsley, Cambridge
Naiad, Holly-leaved
Orchid, Early Spider
Orchid, Fen
Orchid, Ghost
Orchid, Late Spider
Orchid, Lizard
Orchid, Military
Orchid, Monkey
Pear, Plymouth
Pennyroyal
Pink, Cheddar
Pink, Childing
Pigmyweed
Ragwort, Fen
Ramping-fumitory, Martin's
Restharrow, Small
Rock-cress, Alpine
Rock-cress, Bristol
Sandwort, Norwegian
Sandwort, Teesdale
Saxifrage, Drooping
Saxifrage, Tufted

Solomon's-seal, Whorled
Sow-thistle, Alpine
Spearwort, Adder's-tongue
Speedwell, Fingered
Speedwell, Spiked
Spurge, Purple
Starfruit
Star-of-Bethlehem, Early
Stonewort, Foxtail
Strapwort
Violet, Fen
Viper's-grass
Water-plantain, Ribbon leaved
Wood-sedge, Starved
Woodsia, Alpine
Woodsia, Oblong
Wormwood, Field
Woundwort, Downy
Woundwort, Limestone
Yellow-rattle, Greater